;999

7 999

3
97

1997

|

10

Winning
PR Tactics

■

UMETLO

The Institute of Management (IM) is at the forefront of management development and best management practice. The Institute embraces all levels of management from students to chief executives. It provides a unique portfolio of services for all managers, enabling them to develop skills and achieve management excellence. If you would like to hear more about the benefits of membership, please write to Department P, Institute of Management, Cottingham Road, Corby NN17 1TT. This series is commissioned by the Institute of Management Foundation.

Winning PR Tactics!

Effective Techniques to Boost Your Sales

■

PETER SHELDON GREEN

the Institute
of Management
PITMAN PUBLISHING

PITMAN PUBLISHING
128 Long Acre, London WC2E 9AN

A Division of Longman Group UK Limited

First published in Great Britain 1994

© Peter Sheldon Green, 1994

A CIP catalogue record for this book can be obtained
from the British Library.

ISBN 0 273 60552 6 (Paperback)
ISBN 0 273 607510 (Cased)

Photoset in Linotron Century Schoolbook by
Northern Phototypesetting Co. Ltd, Bolton
Printed and bound in Great Britain
by Bell and Bain Ltd, Glasgow

*The Publishers' policy is to use paper manufactured
from sustainable forests.*

Contents

∎

v

Acknowledgements

■

Nobody can write a technical or management book of this type without owing a debt to a large number of people. I would like to acknowledge at least some of them with gratitude.

Nigel Ellis, doyen of the PR industry and involved in three first class books on PR, put me right on various errors at the synopsis stage of writing, and will so strongly disagree with some of my views that I didn't dare show him the final text!

All of my colleagues at Sheldon Communications Ltd. shared their views and experience – in particular Martin Balls provided numerous operational check lists and Elizabeth Williamson researched sources of information.

David Cunliffe and William Comery helped to develop an approach to PR which extends beyond this book and into the real world of PR practice.

While recognising their, and many others', help I should clearly state that the responsibility for views expressed and for any errors or omissions is entirely mine.

Introduction

■

Public relations has become an important part of the marketing and corporate thinking of many companies. A term which would hardly have been recognised by most people some 30 years ago has become commonplace. A considerable industry of PR specialists has grown up throughout the world, with the USA and the UK probably in the lead.

Along with this growth PR has become ever more respectable. The pattern in the UK is typical. PR people have taken to calling themselves 'professionals', established examination criteria to qualify as a 'Member of the Institute of Public Relations', charge out their time at levels roughly equivalent to lawyers and accountants and invented a whole new sub-language to cloak their craft in mystery and give it added status.

Of course PR people are not unique in this. The invention of a semi-private language has always been an early requirement of any profession. Doctors and lawyers recognised this long before marketing consultants, PR experts or systems analysts were even dreamed of. There is some justification for this. There *are* some activities and some concepts which need a special vocabulary to describe them. Unfortunately the effect of such specialist jargon is to exclude understanding from anyone who is not part of the initiated group. It makes complicated that which is straightforward and makes opaque that which is clear. At the end of the day most of the practice of PR is very valuable but it simply isn't that complex.

Public relations is an important discipline in the running of a company – it can lead to increased sales and profits; it can greatly help an organisation in its relationships with customers, suppliers, legislators and staff; it can offer some protection against attacks on a company's reputation.

This importance is reflected in the increasing degree to which PR practitioners are at the centre of decision processes in industry and business. They sit on the board; they have the ear of the chief executive; and they form an important part of company policy relating to communications. But for every PR action which relates to corporate positioning there are probably a hundred requirements for straightforward marketing support at product level, designed to increase customer awareness and hence sales.

The basis of a great deal of PR practice is simply common sense allied to an awareness of a number of simple rules. Building up the amount of factual information on which a PR practitioner relies takes time. Acquiring contacts takes time. Gaining experience takes time. Understanding the principles of PR practice is, however, relatively easy to achieve.

The aim of this book is to demystify the business of public relations and set out the basic skills which are used. It does not attempt to be a substitute for a proper training in the discipline. Rather it is an attempt to make the thinking and the techniques of the modern PR operator less opaque, to make it easier to manage PR people, whether in house or in a consultancy, and, to a limited extent, make it possible to do a competent basic job for oneself.

Inevitably the book concentrates on the more straightforward aspects and most easily acquired techniques of PR with a consequent over-emphasis on PR used for product or service support and with media relations being treated as by far the most important single element. This is not the way the PR professional community would wish to present itself, nor is it a fair reflection of the way that PR programmes may be run at any kind of sophisticated level – both by consultants and by in-house practitioners. Nonetheless it accurately reflects, or so I firmly believe, the greatest part of PR activity carried out in the UK (with an even greater emphasis on media relations in many, if not all, other countries).

It is not the intention to minimise the level of skills and

knowledge which are available from PR professionals (in 1992 the Institute of Public Relations introduced a fairly stiff examination criterion for membership, though the vast majority of current members joined before this requirement was enacted). It is, however, the intention to point out that a great deal of PR can be effectively done without a long and elaborate training – rather in the same way that one needs a qualified accountant to conduct an audit but book keeping can be handled in a variety of perfectly satisfactory ways.

PR people take themselves very seriously, and so they should. PR is an important and valuable discipline for any company and a legitimate management function. It would, however, be a great shame if managers believed that managing one's PR is an exclusive function of senior management in large organisations, or that creating a planned PR programme is only appropriate for such organisations.

x

The techniques of planning and implementing a planned PR programme discussed in the following chapters relate most directly to commercial organisations and are orientated fairly heavily to the use of PR as a marketing or sales support discipline. However, everything that is said in this commercial context has application to non-commercial contexts, for example the requirements of local government or the needs of charities.

In the same way any discussion of PR as applied to large organisations is similarly appropriate, though on a lesser scale, to smaller organisations. For example the discussion of how to set up a PR programme and the steps which one needs to take to ensure that what one is doing is both relevant and cost-effective applies just as much to small organisations as it does to large ones. The same steps should be followed and the same management structure adopted even though it may sometimes be possible to set out the programme on a couple of sides of A4 paper, rather than in a multi-paged report.

If one brings a degree of discipline to one's thinking about PR and what it can offer in the way of benefits and if one carries this discipline through to the implementation of a thought-out programme, then it will be a very unusual organisation indeed which cannot benefit from a deliberate effort to manage its public relations. One needs to do this on a scale which is appropriate to the organisation's size and needs and one needs to allocate proper resources to the task. However, such resources need not be as extensive as one might suppose and, for much of the time, do not demand an unrealistically high level of experience and training.

There is, however, a great deal to know if one is a full-time PR professional and no book, even one many times the length of this one, could hope to cover everything. Some areas have been treated with a degree of detail simply because they are those most likely to be of concern in a normal working PR environment and some areas merely touched on because they start to move into the realm of the unusual or the specialist. The disciplines of public affairs, investor relations and crisis management are consequently dealt with extremely briefly on the basis that anything more than the barest outline would be very misleading if not expanded into an entire book.

The approach adopted has, therefore, been to try to set out the basic principles which govern the various activities which make up the greater part of what we normally understand by the term 'public relations', and at the same time talk, in a fairly unstructured way, about particular considerations or tips of the trade which may be of value.

The intention is to provide a framework for thinking and some direct pieces of practical advice. At the same time it is hoped that the fairly informal discussion will set off trains of thought or spark ideas which are at least as valuable as the specific information contained within the text of the book.

Chapters have been organised so that it should prove possible to go to any particular chapter for advice on any particular aspect of PR work and gain at least a basic understanding of what is involved. Also, since it is a recurring theme of the book that much work is a matter of following a few rules and sourcing essential information, there is a chapter devoted to information sources – with some comment on their usefulness. I very much hope that the book will, thus, work as a practical work aid as well as operating as a general discussion of the subject of PR.

It is not the intention to suggest that there is no role for 'professional' PR people in the practice of public relations, on the contrary, it is very clear that they have a great deal to offer. It is the intention to suggest that, just as you don't need a doctor for every little ache and pain, there's a fair bit of home medicine which can be applied to the practice of managing one's public relations.

PR is an accessible discipline and a 'do it yourself' approach may often prove to be an appropriate one. Even where the scale and complexity of programmes does require expert input, either bought in from outside consultants or by employing 'in house' professionals, an understanding of the basic principles and techniques employed is not particularly difficult to acquire – with obvious benefits for effective management of the PR function even if one is not oneself a PR professional.

PR exists, like it or not

The question is sometimes asked, 'Should we have public relations?' Posed in this way, it's a damfool question. Any organisation, whatever its business, has public relations simply by virtue of existing.

The people who buy your goods or services have an impression of you and what you have to offer; so do the people who know of you but do not buy from you; so do your suppliers; so do your employees; so do your competitors and so, indeed, does everyone with whom you come in contact. These groups are an organisation's publics and every single one of them enters into a relationship, passive or active, with that organisation. They perceive an organisation in a particular way. They have a view of you.

These views are formed by a whole range of factors over and above the quality and price of the goods or services which you have on offer. Everything from the way in which an organisation's telephone is answered through to what has, or hasn't, been written about you in the press affects the way in which people regard you.

There will be a number of 'publics' (more about these later – see Chapter 6) who relate to an organisation and who have varying degrees of awareness, understanding and, frequently quite unfounded, views about that organisation. This happens whether one likes it or not and, whether one likes it or not, the perceptions which are formed are subject to revision and to change.

It is not a matter of choice whether one has a reputation or not.

The choice is whether one should take conscious action to manage that reputation. This means deliberately setting out to influence the perceptions of those groups of people who are important to one's business.

Of course every organisation does this to some extent, even if it hasn't formally recognised the fact. It may not be described as public relations but when the switchboard is instructed to answer the 'phone politely, when a salesman smiles on encountering a customer, when it's decided to update the letterhead, when a trade journalist is sent a sales catalogue in response to a query, then an effort is being made to influence opinion over and above the simple provision of products and services.

Put at its crudest, almost everyone understands that if you're dealing with someone who likes you, or at least someone who can appreciate your point of view, then things are likely to go a great deal more smoothly. If you can change an unfavourable impression to a favourable one, or create an awareness of your existence where there was previously ignorance, then nothing but benefit can result.

People prefer to buy products which they have heard of to products which are completely unknown to them. They prefer to buy products which they have heard of in a positive context to those which they are merely aware of. Precisely the same applies to organisations which they deal with as it does to individual products. People come to have heard of products, organisations or whatever in a whole variety of ways and they come to form impressions, negative or positive, in a similarly wide variety of ways.

These opinion forming factors are not random. They include such obvious sales messages from an organisation as advertising and sales literature. They also include impressions formed less directly through such items as press reporting, word of mouth, exhibitions, conferences, newsletters, etc.

This may seem like kindergarten stuff but it isn't. Once it's recognised that opinions are formed and may be modified in different ways and for different reasons and that, to some extent at least, these opinion-forming factors can be managed, then it becomes a very real question as to whether it's worth investing time, effort and money in developing and running a programme designed specifically to influence the way an organisation is perceived by the people who matter to it.

The question is not whether opinion can be influenced. It quite clearly can, as has been demonstrated time and again by the successful application of PR techniques in virtually every walk of life. The question is much more one of how far opinion can be influenced coupled with how difficult such influencing is likely to be.

As with most questions of management it finally comes down to a matter of money. Obviously it's desirable that one should be thought well of but if the cost of setting out to influence opinion, over and above routine activities of an organisation, is greater than the benefits which will be obtained then it's not worth doing. On the other hand if the benefit of actively managing one's PR exceeds the cost of such activity then it would be foolish not to put such a programme in place.

Unfortunately such a cost benefit analysis is never easy to do. PR does not make sales, it creates an atmosphere in which sales are more likely to be made. Similarly in virtually every area of PR practice it acts as an influencer and facilitator – crisis management PR does not prevent the crisis, rather it is an exercise in damage limitation after a crisis; employee relations activity does not achieve a single successful negotiation on works practice, rather it makes it more likely that satisfactory agreement will be reached; effective community relations PR does not obtain a single planning consent, rather it makes it more likely that such consents may be obtained etc.

A consequence of the indirect way in which PR operates is that its effectiveness cannot be measured directly by simple observation – rather its influence needs to be assessed by specialist efforts such as comparative attitude research which tend to be

3

both expensive and time consuming.

The principle that a PR programme must deliver in benefit more than it costs may, in practice, still come down to a judgement call when deciding whether or not to implement a formal PR programme. No matter what systems are put in to measure effectiveness, and such systems are possible, there will always be a subjective element in deciding if, and how much, to invest. Part of such judgement should also take into account the cost of *not* having a formal programme.

We've already seen that it's not a question of whether or not one has PR but rather whether one should manage it rather than just let it happen by itself. The failure to manage may not just mean missed opportunities to gain benefit but may also mean damage to reputation which results from failure to act. This isn't just true of major areas such as crisis or issue management. It can be true at quite a basic level.

Let's consider, for example, what happens when a leading trade journal runs, as they do, a special supplement covering the particular area in which an organisation is involved. The journal puts together its editorial content on the basis of information obtained from the industry. It will research some of this itself but will be largely dependent on information received. If one does not provide such information in a suitable and convenient form then it is unlikely that any editorial will result. The supplement will appear, purporting to cover an industry sector, and you won't be mentioned. Now this isn't simply an opportunity lost. Your very absence says something negative if only by implication. If you're not there then you're not important enough, or there's nothing interesting to say about you.

So the effort which would have been required to make sure that you knew about the supplement and provided relevant information should not be measured simply by what one gained from being written about but also by what one stood to lose by being ignored.

4

This is a fairly simplistic example, and doesn't even start to consider whether you should have advertised in the supplement or relative cost effectiveness of an ad as opposed to editorial, but it does, I hope, underline two points:

- PR happens, reputations are created and impressions formed whether or not it is managed
- when one decides not to manage one's PR one does not simply miss opportunities to enhance reputation but also risks avoidable damage.

Deciding to establish a managed PR programme starts from this very simple proposition: 'Will I benefit from this to a degree justified by the cost?' and although the benefit may be difficult to quantify with a high degree of accuracy it should be possible to make a fairly reasoned judgement. It's also possible to take a decision on just how much of one's inevitable PR it's sensible to manage and, consequently, how much one wishes to invest.

5

PR covers a multitude of activities normally, but not always, described by the word 'relations' or 'management' and ranging across techniques and target audiences. Thus some of the products offered by the PR business are: Media Relations, Government Relations, Corporate Relations, Investor Relations, Employee Relations, Crisis Management, Issue Management, Event Management, Bid/Defence Management, Presentation Management, Communications Audit, Sponsorship . . . the list goes on but you don't need to buy the whole shop.

Deciding what you do and don't need in the way of PR management is the first, critical, step in ensuring that any programme put in place will be cost effective. At the end of the day all of the various items on the PR shopping list are merely variations on a theme. They have in common that they wish to present an organisation, or a product, or a service or, even, an individual in the best possible light to people whose goodwill is of value. The various labels simply describe the groups of people to be influenced or the means of exercising influence. As long as one remembers that such lists represent useful ways of dividing up the various PR options for ease of consideration then they have some value. They should not be allowed to make things more complicated by being treated as a specialist jargon – they're just labels for ease of reference.

It would be naive in the extreme to pretend that there are no areas of PR practice which require highly developed skills or that the range and sophistication of techniques employed by PR people has not grown hugely over the years – not least because PR has become integrated with mainstream company activities which demand much stricter disciplines then was expected of the early publicists, be they advertising people or PROs.

Nonetheless, the fundamental aims of PR have not changed significantly since its recognition as a discipline in its own right. Whether the definition adopted is 'the engineering of consent' or the Institute of Public Relations' rather formal 'the deliberate, planned and sustained effort to establish and maintain mutual understanding between an organisation and its publics', it comes down to deciding what you want to say, who you want to say it to and how you can make sure they hear you.

Successfully managed PR achieves this more cost effectively and usually more believably than advertising, more widely than personal contact and more rapidly than word of mouth.

2

What do we really mean by PR?

We mentioned a couple of offered definitions of public relations in the last chapter and in looking at what the term is generally taken to mean we can do worse than start with the Institute of Public Relations formulation, tinkered with on a number of occasions since its first expression but never really bettered: *'Public relations practice is defined . . . as the planned and sustained effort to establish and maintain goodwill and mutual understanding between an organisation and its publics'* (the word 'public' became pluralised some decades after the first formulation with the rather belated recognition that an organisation will have more than one distinct audience for its messages, with different interests and rather different requirements for mutual understanding). As definitions go it may lack something in snappiness but it does get to the heart of what PR is all about. It is about relationships and perceptions and, ideally, making these work for, rather than against you.

In many ways PR practice in this sense has been around as far as human records go back, though its aim tended to be political rather than commercial. Much of the literature from Roman times can be seen to have a clear purpose of establishing goodwill, or ill will, and mutual understanding in addition to its apparent purpose of providing a history of the Gallic wars or whatever. Even Shakespeare's history plays may be seen as PR exercises in legitimising the claims of the House of Tudor and underpinning the notion of the divine right of kings.

In more recent times, however, credit for the introduction of planned PR practice is frequently given to an American called Ivy Lee. Lee recognised that there were occasions where good-will was best obtained by being open and honest about facts, even where these facts were not entirely in one's favour. He applied this insight to the nascent American railways whose reaction to crashes and accidents, often occurring miles from any centre of civilisation, was to cover up, conceal details and refuse to give any information. The result was that the public became alarmed, believed rail travel was extremely dangerous, hated the railroad owners, started to avoid railway travel and lobbied against land acquisition by the railroad companies.

Lee changed all this. He ensured that full details of accidents, including the names of those killed or injured, were made public and provided rapidly to relatives. At the same time he explained how accidents had occurred and placed newspaper articles putting deaths on the railways into perspective – comparing the safety of passenger miles travelled by rail with pedestrian miles in downtown New York, for example. The results were dramatic, or at least that's how the story goes. The public sympathised with the railway companies, understood their operating difficulties, appreciated their relative safety and, eventually, enshrined them in the Great American Dream. No small achievement for the publishing of some lists at railway stations, issuing a few press releases and under-standing the power of planned public relations.

Lee is also credited with persuading an early Rockefeller to fill his pockets with coppers whenever he went out and throw them to passing urchins, thus transforming his image from plutocratic exploiter of the poor to munificent merchant prince!

The stories about Lee may well be apocryphal. It is not a matter of anecdote but of fact that in this century the basic skills which make up the PR operator's armoury became largely developed as a result of the two world wars. The fairly crude propaganda exercises and 'Hun bashing' stories placed in the British and American press developed into a far subtler and organised operation targeted at a variety of different publics and carrying a range of messages.

Persuading the British public not merely to eat butter substitutes but to enjoy them, winning the support and sympathy of a still neutral American public, explaining the whole range of activities on the home front which were important to the war effort, all demanded the development of PR skills. These skills, and practitioners who knew how to use them, became available for deployment in the commercial world once Britain returned to peacetime. It is no accident that the PR industry became a cogent entity in the UK in the post-Second World War years, nor that Britain has the most developed PR industry in Europe – though, of course, this is not to be explained solely in terms of the wartime role of Government Information Officers.

Coincidental with the development of a PR industry has been the explosion in information technology and the mechanical ability for organisations to communicate more easily, more quickly and more accurately to more people and more groups of people.

9

It has become far easier to target particular messages to particular groups of people. It has become far easier to disseminate information rapidly and widely. There has been an exponential growth in the demand for information and a parallel growth in people prepared to supply it. The PR operator's problem has ceased to be one of how to get information out and become one of how to distinguish his particular message or view point from the babble of competing voices all demanding attention.

We do live in a global village. Events which occur in London are known about in Tokyo or New York within minutes if not seconds. We have the means to communicate almost instantaneously across large portions of the globe and every one of us is habitually absorbing more information from more separate sources than at any time in history.

All this is very exciting and at a macro level means the potential power of planned PR, and the potential downside of not managing one's PR, has increased enormously. At a more down to earth level it means that it has become possible to manage PR programmes far more effectively and to make things happen much more quickly.

In the important area of media relations it used to be the case that who you knew was always more important than what you knew. This no longer holds true. Contacts will always be extremely valuable, and in some cases still be the vital link in a PR operation. In general, however, news gathering has moved a long way from private briefings based on personal acquaintance and anyone with a strong story to tell has the means to tell it and, through a proliferation of reference books and databases, the knowledge of who to tell it to.

The same is true in virtually every area of PR operation. Identifying, contacting and briefing analysts as part of an investor relations programme, for example, is much more easily understood and achieved than used to be the case and there is a greater demand for information from those analysts; but there are also more companies competing for their attention through formal investor relations programmes. Similarly, there is greater formality and control over the way in which one can make one's case to Parliament, both British and European, and wider access to opinion-formers within Government and the Civil Service; but there are more people with well-prepared Government relations programmes, often operated through specialist lobby firms.

The pattern repeats itself through specialist print work, corporate sponsorship, speaker opportunities, issue management and all the other activities which may go to make up a managed PR programme. Accessibility of information and technical innovations in all aspects of communications have resulted in a greatly increased potential for running effective PR programmes. However, hand-in-hand with this has gone an increased awareness of the power of planned PR and consequently an increased number of PR practitioners competing for what is, at the end of the day, a finite market for information.

Increasingly PR practitioners have recognised this and have responded by defining key target audiences for PR messages more tightly and by aiming their efforts to 'establish and maintain goodwill and mutual understanding' to clearly defined groups – a rifle rather than a shot-gun approach to all but the most generalised PR activities which may be aimed at the public at large. At the same time they have refined the means of disseminating these messages – extending the simple concept of media relations to a wide range of communications techniques.

From this increasingly analytical approach has developed a whole range of 'disciplines', specialities and, of course, jargon. *But the fundamental principles of PR practice remain simple.* In fact the availability of readily accessed information on who's who in one's target audiences, who's who in the media, and what other communications channels are open to one, coupled with greatly increased ease in the physical distribution of PR messages, has actually made the PR operator's job easier in the sense that a competent job can be done purely by drawing on this available information and by following a number of largely common sense rules.

None of this means that there is no longer any need for flair in PR, nor does it mean that there is no requirement for particular skills and knowledge for particular operations, nor, indeed, does it mean that experience is of no value. What it does mean is that, given a reasonable degree of intelligence and application, a fairly basic PR job can be done by almost anybody prepared to take it seriously enough to make a real effort. There will be occasions when a fairly basic job is all that is required. There will also be times when more than a simple, and fairly crude, dissemination of information is needed and this is the time when one should no more think of being one's own PR man than think of being one's own doctor.

Because the fundamental activity which makes up a typical PR campaign turns out to be as much a matter of common sense and simple rules as anything, there is a danger that one will believe that it is trivial or unimportant. Nothing could be further from the truth. Effective PR management has the potential to impinge on an organisation's profit and performance as much as any other management discipline. It needs to be planned, thought through and carried out with attention to detail and, contrary to some popular belief, can be very hard work. It is not, however, devastatingly difficult to understand what PR is or how it operates. It may well be that PR professionals, seeing that some managers equate 'understandable' with 'trivial' have, deliberately or not, complicated the subject. In doing so they have done a disservice both to PR practitioners and to managers whose jobs ought to include an appreciation and, possibly, employment of managed public relations.

In some ways the whole business of PR has taken on the same, slightly sinister, glamour which the advertising industry had in the 1960s. A belief arose, fuelled by books like *The Hidden Persuaders*, that here was an industry which was capable of making us, Joe Public, do and think in a particular way without our being aware of it. This feeling, fuelled by the coining of terms like 'spin doctor' and by various revelations of nefarious doings by PR men, has transferred itself to PR. At a trivial level this view is valid, at least to the extent that our knowledge of the world, of political policies, of products and even of people whom we haven't met is filtered to us via various communications channels, primarily the so called media. Without question, PR operatives seek to influence the media, manipulate it even.

In reality, however, this influence is confined to ensuring that one's message has a chance to be heard by people who might be interested in it. If two companies launch similar products at around the same time and one takes the trouble to inform the relevant press about what it has done and the other doesn't, then it's hardly surprising that one will receive editorial mention and the other won't. It's hardly surprising that one company will gain more interest in its new product as a result of this press relations activity. And it's very likely that the company which sent out the press release will, all things being equal, achieve more sales. The media has not been manipulated. Nothing sinister or unethical has been done. But it would be hard to claim that the media has not, in some sense, been used. And this would be equally true if one company had sent out a better written press release, accompanied by a more interesting photograph, to journalists it had taken the trouble to cultivate than its competitor.

Effective public relations in support of one's product or, for that matter, one's point of view will not alter the merits of the product or the point of view. What it will do is make it more likely that one's product, point of view or whatever, is better understood and is given more sympathetic consideration in any decision which relates to it, whether that decision be to buy, to vote, to apply for a job or any other action.

Provided one does not have unrealistic expectations of what PR can and cannot achieve and provided one is prepared to take time (and effective PR can be very time-consuming) it is theoretically possible for almost anyone with a sound understanding of his or her business to design and implement a PR programme without calling in specialist 'professional' help. Such a programme may be confined to specific areas of a business' PR needs, may be a little more clumsy in execution than is ideal and may be very consuming of management resources – but it can be done.

In practice what is most likely to prove of real value is to understand the basic techniques of PR, its potential and its limitations, and on the basis of this knowledge be in a position to manage an effective programme which may be delegated totally within an organisation or which may draw on the strengths of external experts for support where their knowledge, experience and contacts are of genuine value.

PR is not a cheap alternative to advertising or direct marketing in the field of product support, rather it is an additional string to the marketing bow which doesn't make sales but which creates an atmosphere in which sales are made more easily. PR at corporate level is not an alternative to good company practice, rather it is a way to ensure that one gets the best possible reputation which one deserves. PR is not something to hide behind when things go wrong, rather it is a way of ensuring

13

that damage to relationships and reputation is kept to a minimum in such circumstances. PR will not make a talentless person any more talented, but it will make sure that what talent there is gets recognised.

So one should not be unrealistic in one's expectations of what one can gain from managing one's PR effectively. But, having said this, it is also true that there are many, many occasions when effective use of PR can deliver a return on investment – in terms of increased sales, influence on legislation, improved staff relations, management of share price etc – which makes the outlay of time and money on PR activity seem paltry compared with other ways of achieving the same results.

The Institute of Public Relations' definition of PR, set out near the start of this chapter, has stood the test of time. Despite various changes, addenda and alternatives from the Institute it remains substantially as it was first formulated. Would that the continually developing way to do the job could be laid out as succinctly!

14

These first two chapters have been mainly concerned with putting PR practice into some sort of context, together with an attempt to debunk some of the pompous and obscurist attitudes which PR has adopted over the last few decades. The body of this book will concern itself with the practical questions of: what to do, how to do it, who should do it and is it worth it?

PR in the marketing mix

Managing one's public relations can be an activity which affects and impinges on virtually every aspect of an organisation's operations. Some of the different aspects of PR activity (government relations, investor relations, employee relations) are dealt with fairly briefly in later chapters of this book and each of these specialist areas has its own particular considerations. Within commercial organisations, however, a major, if not the main, thrust of PR activity is likely to be directed towards product or services marketing, either directly or indirectly.

While the PR techniques and procedures which are discussed in the main body of the book have applications across the range of 'publics' with which an organisation has contact, they are all directly relevant to considerations of PR as a marketing communications support activity – 'marcoms' as it has become widely known, particularly in a business-to-business context. This is the area of PR work which can be seen, most obviously, as contributing to an organisation's profits and it is the type of PR work which is most easily justified in terms of budget spend. It is not surprising that marketing PR is often the first form of planned PR activity to which an organisation commits itself.

To suggest that PR activity is confined to marketing support would be misleading and would be to greatly understate the importance and status which public relations has within an organisation. Indeed, on occasion, public relations considerations established at a corporate level may run directly counter to marketing priorities. However, PR has a significant role to play in the marketing communications of any organisation and planned PR activity is, or should be, an integral part of the marketing mix. Any organisation which does not appreciate this is almost certainly missing opportunities. The operation of managed public relations as a marketing support function is also probably the type of PR work which most readily lends itself to implementation 'in house' and by people who do not work as full-time PR operators.

When PR management is applied as a marketing discipline, in common with all other elements which make up the marketing programme, it is important that it should not be treated in isolation but is seen as an integral element of the marketing mix. This means that there needs to be a clear understanding of how PR integrates with other sales and marketing activities to provide support and reinforcement.

A somewhat simplistic description of what happens is that the role of PR is to create a generalised acceptance of one's product or service; the role of advertising is to exhort potential customers to buy; the role of sales is to convert this combination of goodwill and sales message into an actual sale. With all three elements working together then the chances of a successful sale are greatly increased.

Of course it rarely works quite as simply as this. The sales chain is much more complex where intermediate retailers and distributors are involved. The functions of PR and advertising overlap, as, in the case of direct marketing, do the functions of advertising and sales. A crude lumping together of above and below the line advertising as if they are one and the same thing is not just oversimplification, but actually misleading. No consideration is given to additional marketing communications activity, such as exhibition participation, distributor incentives, product promotions and special offers etc.

Even so, the crude description is valid to the extent that it shows that these simple elements of the marketing communications mix will be much more effective if they are planned to work together. A number of obvious, but frequently ignored, rules which should apply the use of PR as a marketing tool follow from this:

- PR messages must be wholly consistent with advertising and sales messages (too often PR activity is driven by a wish to gain exposure, usually in the press, with insufficient consideration of whether such exposure has real value in a marketing, or indeed corporate, context)

- the timing of product PR ('product PR' is a term often used to describe the type of PR work used in marketing support) initiatives should be determined by the overall timing of marketing activity – always allowing for the relatively long lead times which PR typically requires to produce results

- target audiences for PR messages should be determined by marketing needs, not by PR convenience

- in deciding on marketing communications plans there needs to be an awareness of the potential PR consequences and possible benefits which result from other activity as well as an awareness of purely PR driven possibilities (a good example of this being done well is provided in the UK by Häagen Dazs ice cream where a provocatively sensual advertising campaign for the product was used as a basis for a PR campaign which generated vastly more exposure than the advertising itself – and all coverage, both advertising and editorial, was totally consistent with the product's market positioning).

17

All this is plain common sense, but these very simple considerations are frequently ignored. All too often PR is grafted on to an already finalised programme and the inputs of PR practitioners come too late to be given proper weight. Moreover insufficient time is left to allow the PR programme to be properly planned and implemented as a synchronised part of the overall programme.

There are a number of reasons why this may happen but one suspects that it is usually quite simply the power of budgets. By and large, PR is a relatively inexpensive element in a marcoms programme – particularly when compared to advertising. It's natural enough that if one is spending ten times as much on advertising as on PR then one gives priority in one's thinking to the bigger area of spend. Natural enough it may be, but it's mistaken. To some extent the relative cheapness of PR is a reflection of the fact that, for some tasks and at comparatively low budget levels, PR is hugely more cost effective than advertising – the level of spend is not a good indication of importance. It is also the case that advertising and PR are complementary, not competing, activities and each needs to be managed with a clear strategy and programme of activity. Treating the two disciplines similarly from planning stage onwards and ensuring that an integrated approach is adopted can only result in better results.

(This matter of budgets is sometimes allowed to influence the weight given to the thoughts of outside advisors where they are used. Thus an ad agency's views may be given much more weight than a PR consultant's. Again this may well be mistaken and it's worth remembering that an ad agency earns some 15 per cent of the money spent with it, the rest going on production and the cost of space, whereas a PR consultancy may well earn almost all of its gross income as retained fees. Thus on a spending ratio of 7:1 the level of executive time and thought which an ad agency and a PR firm will commit to a client's business should be virtually the same.)

In practice, the importance which is placed on PR as part of the marketing mix will vary very considerably from organisation to organisation and this variation will be partly a reflection of the organisation's type of business and partly a reflection of the particular style of marketing management. This is as it should be, provided the balance is one which has been thought about and not one which has been arrived at through inertia or accident. Really effective marketing communications activity may contain a very large PR element or a relatively small one. It is unlikely, however, to ignore PR altogether.

An illustration of this might be the contrasting approaches of two different types of consumer products companies in the UK, Body Shop and Mars Confectionery.

Body Shop does no media advertising at all but, as part of its overall approach, has made maximum use of a whole range of public relations techniques to support its extremely successful retailing operation. Mars pays careful attention to PR, particularly at a corporate level, but in terms of product support its PR activity is minuscule compared with its huge advertising spend. Both organisations are very successful in their different ways and both enjoy a high reputation with their customer base. The different approach to marcoms activity simply reflects their very different approaches and cultures. However when Body Shop do advertise, and they have done a little in the USA, or when Mars does commit to PR initiatives, and their triumphant sponsorship of the London Marathon was an example of product PR commitment, then the messages are totally consistent between PR and advertising.

Although the balance may vary it is not normally a question of either or when one considers advertising and PR. If it were then PR would win hands down on the basis of cost alone. Rather they are two elements in a marketing programme which complement and reinforce each other. There is overlap, for example corporate advertising of the type run by some of the larger utilities might reasonably be described as a PR exercise and some product editorial gained through press relations work within a PR programme performs the same role as advertising but with the additional weight of editorial credibility. This overlap should not, however, be taken to treat the two as alternatives. Most of the time a balanced marketing programme will make use of both advertising and PR and in any cost-conscious programme the PR element will be made to work very hard indeed.

19

To summarise, then: public relations considerations go well beyond purely marketing support needs, which I hope will become very clear from the discussion of the value of reputation in the next chapter. Nevertheless PR has an extremely effective part to play as a marketing support activity. The role of PR within marketing is one which makes it important that public relations work is fully integrated with other marketing communications disciplines and is taken fully into account at early stages of planning. If this is done then the PR element of marcoms is relatively inexpensive, extremely cost effective and results in the other elements of the marketing mix having a better chance of achieving their aims effectively.

4

What price reputation?

'**M**utual understanding and goodwill' may be conveniently expressed in the single word 'reputation'. Reputation is a valuable asset to any organisation and it is with reputation that public relations is mainly concerned. In the last chapter we were primarily concerned with PR operating as a support to the marketing function by raising awareness of a product or service's qualities and benefits. In doing this what PR is setting out to do is to build, or sometimes to protect, the reputation of those products and services. In reality, though, maintaining the reputation of a product, service, individual or organisation may well have a significance which extends well beyond acting as a sales support activity.

It's difficult to place an exact value on something as intangible as the notion of reputation but, quite clearly, if we could arrive at some sort of a figure, albeit a ball park estimate, then we would be some way towards deciding what level of resource should be directed towards building and protecting it.

Before looking at possible ways of arriving at a valuation, however, it is worth considering just how and why it is that some organisations have reputations which are clearly of huge benefit and commercial value to them whereas others, not significantly different in operation, do not.

It would be too strong to claim that an organisation's reputation or the reputation of its products is a consequence simply of how successful it is at managing its public relations. But it is not as far off the mark as one might think at first sight.

The reputation of an organisation's products and services will be based on how good those products and services are. Similarly the reputation of the organisation itself will be based on the quality of its business practices and of its performance. It is unlikely in the extreme that fundamentally bad products will have a good reputation or that an organisation with sloppy business practices, poor record of performance and bad employee relations will be well thought of. However it is quite possible for an organisation to enjoy a higher reputation than is strictly justified by the facts or for its products to be similarly over rated. It is also quite common for reputations to be lower than they deserve from a purely objective standpoint.

How can this be?

It is because of the fact that although reputation is related to quality this relationship is a contingent one. Reputation is not a function of hard facts but is a function of how those facts are perceived. If everyone was in possession of total information, no false information and a capability of making totally objective judgements all the time then, yes, reputation would be an accurate reflection of fact. In practice people are uninformed, part informed, ill informed. Judgements are not objective but are subject to a whole rag bag of preconceptions and prejudices imported from all sorts of sources.

For anyone with whom an organisation has contact its reputation is based on a mishmash of information, some accurate and some not, all of which is filtered through a set of preconditioned attitudes. As we noted earlier any organisation, any brand, any public individual has public relations like it or not. It is when we attempt to manage these relationships through, among other things, ensuring a flow of positive information and minimising negative information and attempting to address pre-conditioned attitudes which may be unhelpful, that one is engaged in managed PR. It is this activity, just as much as the underlying truths, which will create and sustain reputation.

Of course it is not just those activities which we group together under the title of 'PR' which act in this way. Every aspect of communication has a role in building and sustaining reputation from advertising through to personal contact. But a significant element in the building of reputation and an even greater element in protecting it from threat is directly attributable to how well one manages one's formal PR activity.

What is very clear is that bad PR can destroy or badly damage a reputation which has taken years to build virtually overnight and, on occasion, this can happen purely as a result of bad publicity, with no real underlying cause or change of circumstances. An example of this is the now legendary speech by Gerald Ratner to the Institute of Directors where his 'we sell crap' comment and the way that it was widely reported in the press badly damaged the jewellery chain's credibility and sales although the company had done nothing wrong and its product range and pricing was still the same as had established Ratner's as Britain's leading High Street jewellery operation.

What applies to companies applies equally to products. The reputation of a product or a brand depends on how it is perceived and, only contingently, on what it is. Given a high reputation it becomes possible not only to sell in greater quantities but also to demand a higher price. A startling example of this is provided by over-the-counter pharmaceutical products. In this market it is perfectly normal for a standard drug to be marketed as a proprietary brand in greater quantities and at a much higher price than its direct generic equivalent. Compare, for example the price of Disprin and soluble aspirin or Nurofen and Ibuprofen. The difference here is, almost exclusively, one of perceptions.

23

If we want to put a value on reputation then what we are seeking to value is the benefit accruing to a company or product from the goodwill which has been created for it. This may sound somewhat tricky but, at least as an approximation, it's fairly straightforward.

Let's consider the 1988 purchase of the confectionery company Rowntree Mackintosh by the Swiss food group Nestlé for £2.55 billion. Rowntree's physical assets in the form of plant and stock accounted for one-fifth of the purchase price, the remaining four-fifths was paid for marketing and production know-how and infrastructure and for Rowntree's reputation in the form of a strong corporate reputation and a string of strong brand names. A similar purchase at around the same time was Phillip Morris' payment of $12.9 million for Kraft, of which only one quarter was represented by physical assets.

In both these cases a very large proportion of the purchase price was paid for the goodwill associated with the companies bought – their reputations. Exactly the same applies where individual brands or product lines are sold by one company to another and where the price invariably exceeds any physical assets involved.

We can make a start on valuing reputation, then, by looking at the difference in market price, assuming a willing buyer/willing seller transaction, and the physical asset value of the business or brand being considered. Of course there doesn't have to be an actual sale, an estimate of what the value of such a transaction would be is perfectly sufficient or, in the case of a quoted company, a simple calculation of its market value can be made from the share price.

The value of reputation contained in a brand can, then, be seen to equal potential buyer's price less value of stock and production facilities. The reputation value of a company may be seen to equal potential buyer's price minus value of physical assets and know-how. This second calculation involves a value judgement on know-how which may vary greatly from company to company.

The calculation is relatively crude, based on assessment and very approximate but it does serve to remind one of just how valuable an asset reputation may be and how, like any other asset, it is vital to protect it and, as far as possible, to increase it.

PR alone will not achieve growth in reputation or protection of reputation. There have to be some fundamental merits in an organisation and its products for any long-term reputation building programme to be successful. However, because reputation is a matter of perception, it follows that good public relations is a necessary, although not sufficient, condition for a good reputation.

One has public relations, like it or not, and it's quite possible for these to be good even where not consciously managed. Reliance on instinct and an ad hoc approach to contact with one's publics may very well work quite adequately for at least some of the time. It does, however, seem somewhat irresponsible to leave something quite so important unmanaged when the cost of doing so is not particularly high and certainly pales into insignificance compared with the value of the asset involved.

All this may seem a bit academic in terms of the sort of activity which is normally carried out as a PR programme. Discussions of the value of reputation may seem a far cry from making sure that everyone who might want to buy one's products knows about them and knows their qualities, or making sure that one's trade association is doing a proper job in protecting against legislation which might damage one's business, or even informing voters what their community tax is being spent on.

Cost/benefit discussion of PR is usually conducted at a much more basic level, and probably rightly so. However, even if the whole notion is simply noted and filed away in the back of one's mind, it is important to take on board the principle involved because an understanding of how important perceptions are leads directly to an understanding of the value of managing one's public relations.

The train of logic runs very simply:

- reputation is an asset of significant value
- reputation is largely a function of perceptions
- perceptions can be influenced
- planned PR activity results in the positive influencing of perceptions
- therefore planned PR activity affects an asset of significant value

- therefore planned PR activity is, itself, an activity of significance.

Despite this perfectly valid argument there is no question that the PR function within organisations is frequently given relatively low priority and its value is underestimated. This undervaluation may well result simply from a confusion between what it is for something to be difficult and what it is for something to be important. The very fact that managing PR is neither that complicated nor that expensive may have led to an assumption that it is, therefore, not important. Such an assumption would be a serious error for most organisations.

5

What do you want to achieve?

The setting of objectives for any management activity is a necessary step towards efficiency which seems too obvious even to bother with. All too often this obvious step is not taken when it comes to looking at PR work.

Far too often PR is ineffective, or less effective than it could be, because nobody seriously has sat down and worked out what benefits it is hoped to gain. Quite clearly if one is trying to carry through a PR programme with no clear aims in view then it is very difficult for that programme to be anything other than unstructured. If you're not clear about what you're trying to do then you have no way of knowing what you're achieving, no way of modifying activity towards particular aims, no way of deciding whether the time and money spent on PR is well or badly spent and, perhaps most importantly, no way of imposing a yardstick of good practice on what is being done.

In such circumstances it's hardly surprising that PR becomes the poor relation of communications activity and is both under-managed and under-funded. The result is inevitably dis-appointment, or of confirming public relations activity in its peripheral position within an organisation's communications programme.

The need to decide clearly what one wishes to achieve does not, in theory, depend on any external factor such as the ability to identify achievement or put a value on it. Theory is one thing, however, and practice another and demonstrable achievement leads to setting new targets while, in contrast, lack of measurable attainment leads to a degree of apathy and low prioritising.

One of the reasons that PR can become marginalised in an organisation's communications activity, particularly its marketing communications, is that PR achievement can be difficult to measure. You can't put a coupon on the bottom of a press release in the same way that you can with a direct mail shot or direct response advertisement and, consequently, measure return on investment (ROI) in immediate terms. You can't measure sales made as a result of PR activity in the same way you can measure the effectiveness of a salesman by calculating his or her total cost against overheads and measuring this against his or her total contribution to earned income.

28

Marketing PR, when it works, will, in fact, result in more responses to direct mail, make the salesperson's job more easy, generate more visitors to your exhibition stand, produce more sales leads and, in general, create an environment in which marketing a product or service becomes easier.

How on earth can one measure such a vague contribution to the overall marketing mix? As a rule you can't make such a measurement directly or you can only do so at a prohibitive cost. You *can* introduce a number of indirect measures to make sure that you are not wasting time and effort on non productive work.

The weaknesses of the most obvious ways of attempting to measure PR effectiveness are worth noting. You can run an analysis of media coverage but this will limit itself to the media relations element of a PR campaign and is likely to be fundamentally flawed as an exercise (what, for example, is the credibility rating of positive editorial coverage against advertising – given the higher credibility of editorial versus the total control of advertising content and, therefore, what value do you place on coverage gained in money terms?). You can measure column centimetres in your target press and try to assess how effective these have been in terms of carrying key target messages and in terms of the value of the particular publications involved (there are computer programmes to help with this, and as a measure purely of media relations effectiveness this approach represents a great improvement on simply counting up column centimetres and trying to make some equivalence with advertising; however, it still only covers media relations work and does not relate achievement back to any financial base. But it does allow measure against pre-set targets if these have been put in place). At a cost which is likely to be higher than the PR programme itself you can engage in a qualitative market research programme aimed at measuring changing attitudes within the target audience. (This type of exercise is obviously expensive and is also flawed because it has to assume that PR work is entirely responsible for such changing attitudes and this is very unlikely to be the true case.) You can track 'white mail' leads which result from PR activity via editorial coverage. This will provide some degree of measure of the effectiveness of PR used as an alternative to direct response advertising. However PR offers so much more than simply generating sales leads and such a measure ignores all other benefits obtained.

None of these various approaches can be treated as a direct measure of the effectiveness of PR, whatever may be claimed for them by PR people desperate to introduce some sort of tangible measure of their craft. They can, however, be used as an indicative measure of how successful specific elements within a programme are, and as such are not without value. The fact that measuring achievement is not perfect is no reason not to institute some form of measurement, while accepting that this will not provide hard, scientific answers but will need to be interpreted using subjective judgements. What is amply clear is that there will be no chance to judge effectiveness if there is no clear aim in view in the first place.

Precisely because it is so very difficult to measure the effectiveness of PR activity it is important to set out very clearly what one hopes to achieve, how one expects to achieve it and how much resource should be put behind it before committing to any planned PR programme.

In deciding what one hopes to achieve it is important that one is realistic in one's expectations. We've already discussed the fact that managed PR will have an influence on attitudes and will raise levels of awareness. It will, as a result, influence decisions but will not force such decisions. It is unreasonable, therefore, to have an expectation that PR will, of itself produce sales.

The objectives for a PR programme will often be set out in terms which may, at first sight, seem unacceptably vague: for example 'raise awareness among potential purchasers of the company's range of products and services', or 'increase understanding of the issue among opinion formers and influencers'. However, such objectives begin to take on a much more precise meaning once they are seen in the context of a planned programme. They will then be able to be seen as providing a basis against which achievement can be assessed, at least at an indicative level.

Taking the two arbitrary examples given above, this is how it might work: let us assume that in the case of 'raise awareness among potential purchasers of the company's range of products and services' it is possible to define these potential purchasers fairly accurately. Let us also assume that it is decided that media relations activity is regarded as the main work to be undertaken.

It then becomes relatively straightforward to identify the key sections of the media which will directly reach this defined group (such a definition might include named trade publications, specialist sections of the business press, specialist newsletters, possibly broadcast programmes) and to ascribe a level of importance to these publications. Once this is done one has a yardstick for measuring the success of one's media relations activity in a way which does not just count column inches but which takes into account the value of the publication concerned and the quality of the information carried. This is precisely the type of measuring which has been mentioned above and for which there are a number of computer programmes available to help in assessment and, provided one makes a clear judgement on the value of target audiences and identification of key messages then this can be an effective way of measuring one part of the PR programme defined by one particular objective – not, it should be noted of the programme overall.

This directing of messages to key audiences through relevant channels is important and should be taken into account both in planning tactics and in measuring success. For a technical product aimed at a specialist audience coverage in, for example, one of the *Financial Times* stable of specialist newsletters may be of considerably more real value than a splash in one of the tabloid newspapers – though much less spectacular.

In the case of 'increase understanding of the issue among opinion formers and influencers' it might well be that the approach is totally different and covers activities such as direct briefings to selected Members of Parliament with an interest in the subject area, meetings with select civil servants, briefing sessions with relevant pressure groups etc.

31

Once again, when one knows what activity is to be undertaken then one is fairly easily able to plan and to measure the effectiveness of the work undertaken. In this case a straight measure of how widely one has been able to cover the known ground and a more subjective assessment of how successful one has been in putting over one's point of view.

In both these examples it should be noted that the measure of success and the setting of objectives relate to specific activities rather than to programmes as a whole. In reality a product support programme is likely to contain a large number of elements beyond media relations (distributor newsletters, exhibition support, conference participation etc). Similarly an issue management programme is likely to incorporate media relations activity, specialist mailings, conference or seminar arrangement and the like.

The pinning down of the programme will always be incomplete unless it takes the form of comparative awareness assessment surveys conducted at regular intervals and these, apart from being very expensive, will measure the total effect of a marketing or promotional programme plus factors totally outside one's control rather than the effectiveness of PR alone.

Setting clear objectives and measuring one's success in achieving them is unlikely ever to be an exact science. What it does is to impose a direction and a discipline on one's PR work which ensures that it will be as effective as one can make it within the resources available. It will also have the effect of setting priorities and avoid wasted effort on unachievable or irrelevant aims.

Too much PR practice relies on an uncritical approach based on a 'feel good' factor both in planning and assessing activity and too often this is used to cloak a lack of effectiveness on the part of PR practitioners.

The need for PR to operate to clear achievement targets is not one which can be seriously queried and in this chapter we have tried to see why this often fails to be the case. Identifying an explanation, essentially the complexity and imprecision of the measurement of results, is not in any way a justification. Indeed the fact that there is some imprecision in assessing achievement makes the setting of targets more, not less, important.

PR management must be subject to the same disciplines as any other activity carried out by an organisation. Every £1 spent, in time, resources or cash, must deliver more than £1 in benefit, direct or indirect. It may not be possible to measure this directly or accurately but in setting objectives and in measuring effectiveness the attempt must be made. Failure to do so is a sure recipe for sloppy thinking, misdirected effort, poor levels of achievement and general wastage of time and effort.

6

Setting up a programme

The bones of what should constitute a PR programme have already been referred to in the preceding chapters. The case has also been made that, particularly because PR is a relatively 'soft' discipline, the need for a formal programme is critical to cost effectiveness and achievement of worthwhile results.

This is all very well as a statement of general principles. We need, however, to pin down just what form such a programme can usefully take, how it might be structured and what it might cover if the idea of a planned, managed and measured approach is going to have any practical value.

Before it is possible even to start setting out a programme of public relations activity it is important to recognise that PR does not operate in a vacuum. The aims and objectives of any PR programme are a reflection of the aims and objectives of an organisation as a whole. The target audiences at whom PR activity should be aimed are either those who have already been identified by an organisation as being critical or they logically follow from an organisation's identified aims. (It is important to recognise that key audiences are not auto- matically identified by an organisation's corporate or mar- keting plan. For example, an organisation which has the broad corporate aim of maintaining its share price within a defined band will target shareholders as being the people who can ensure this is achieved. Analysts, however, will only be identified as a target audience by logically considering who has a major influence on shareholders' and possible shareholders' opinions.)

It also makes a great deal of sense in any programme to know where one is starting from before deciding on where one expects to go, let alone how one expects to get there. Thus it makes absolutely no sense expect to create a programme designed to mould and influence opinion, to inform and raise awareness or whatever if one has no idea what levels of knowledge, what opinions are held in the first place. (For example, setting out to 'raise awareness of an organisation's products and services' will only be effective if one makes sure that one is telling people things which they don't already know and which matter to them. Thus detailed discussion of the range of colours in which a product is available is largely a waste of time if the real interest is in the quality of after sales service; or, at a corporate level, concentrating on showing how good your employee relations are is of little interest if the target public is concerned about your record on environmental pollution.)

34   Well before looking at any programme of activity one needs to put that programme into context. To a considerable extent the specific programme activity will follow logically from such a structure and, although it will not write itself, it becomes far easier to recognise what one should be doing. Equally importantly it will eliminate a whole range of activities which might, at first sight, seem like a good idea but which are largely a waste of time and effort – PR programmes are bedeviled by effort spent on peripheral activities, usually included in the programme because they have not been thought through against defined aims and objectives.

The exercise known as a 'communications audit' has become an accepted preliminary step to developing PR programmes in recent years. It sound complicated but isn't. It simply means going out and talking to representatives of those groups of people who are important to you and finding out what they know, don't know, need to know and, from your point of view, ought to be told. It is, effectively, a piece of market research into attitudes, probably conducted at a qualitative rather than quantitative level, and aimed at your target publics as defined from a PR point of view. It gives you a starting point, if you don't feel confident that you already have one.

Typically a thought-through PR programme will contain the following elements:

- *overview* – putting the PR function into the overall context of an organisation's operations and setting out relevant objectives, mission statements etc, at corporate and marketing levels. This should also include an analysis of the current situation in terms of perceptions and impressions among the organisation's publics and if this cannot be done serious thought should be given to conducting some research prior to going any further with working out a detailed programme.

- *aims and objectives* – specifically related to the PR programme. It should be possible to derive these from the overview.

- *target audiences* – who are the identifiable groups with whom it is of clear value to 'establish mutual understanding and goodwill'?

- *key messages* – what are the key messages which an organisation wishes to get across to these key groups, taking into account what one wishes to say about oneself, what key publics are likely to be interested in hearing and what levels of knowledge, misinformation and bias already exist?

- *strategy* – setting out the overall approach to be adopted and within which the individual tactical elements of the programme should fit. This separation between overall strategy and individual tactics can be an important one if one is to avoid letting activities dictate the form of the programme rather than the overall programme dictating specific activities.

- *tactics/activities* – this is the core of the programme which dictates what will actually be done. While it is upon the degree of success implementing these specific activities that PR is likely to be judged, it is important to recognise that planning the approach and selecting from a range of possible activities is at least as important as the implementation itself.

There are a host of possible techniques which may be

employed, many of which are considered in subsequent chapters, and decisions on which will prove effective must be made in the light of the objectives, strategy, target publics and key messages which have already been identified. A useful discipline in considering possible tactics is to relate each proposed activity back to defined PR objectives. If any proposed activity cannot be seen to relate directly to at least one stated objective then it has no useful part to play within the programme and should not be included.

- *timetable* – it is an important discipline to timetable the programme of activity to be undertaken. Since many PR activities are not geared to particular deadlines it is all too easy to let a programme slip if no proper timetable is in place. Timetabling also ensures that proposed PR initiatives are tied in to other known marketing and communications activities which may be planned and, as we've already argued, it is important to ensure integration and mutual reinforcement between such activities. The sort of fixed events which may need to be taken into account will vary hugely from organisation to organisation and will depend on the role which PR is required to play. They may include such varied events as exhibition participation, issue of interim and final figures, planned price changes, planned advertising or direct mail campaigns, known schedules of Government legislation, plant openings, annual wage negotiations, planned new product range launches, etc. The list goes on and on and it is only by considering one's own specific organisation that a manageable set of fixed points can be determined.

- *costs* – these need to take into account the management cost of running the programme in terms of salaries and associated overheads, or where a consultancy is used in terms of fees, plus the consequential expenses. This expense element will vary very considerably depending on the particular activities undertaken – sponsorship and corporate hospitality, for example, being potentially very costly whereas press relations activity is likely to carry relatively small consequential expenses.

It is worth considering the real cost of executive time, rather than apparent salary cost when considering an 'in house' operation, particularly if a comparison is to be made with the relative cost of employing outside consultants. A very rough rule of thumb is that, typically, any employee at executive level in an organisation is likely to cost something in excess of twice their annual salary to employ, though as with all things this can vary greatly between organisations.

■ *controls* – it is necessary to set up a clear system of controls as part of the programme. This is, of course, necessary in pursuing any programme of activity against a pre-determined plan and timetable. In the case of a PR programme the need is particularly strong because of the tendency to slip against the timetable, as mentioned above; because the activity deadlines within the programme are mainly self imposed; because the very nature of PR is such that the urgent tends to take precedence over the important even more than in other management disciplines, and this is an error to be avoided; because a programme which deals with perceptions rather than hard facts needs to be monitored on a continuing basis and modified as necessary; because the sheer opportunist possibilities which inevitably occur within a PR programme means that continuing control is needed to ensure that the programme is not allowed to slip out of direction by veering away from the prime objectives; and, most important, because without control over who says what, where, when and how, PR initiatives cease to be a programme but simply become a babble of noise.

37

All of this sounds very formal and so it is to the extent that unstructured PR is never going to be as effective as a planned programme. Just how elaborate and all encompassing a PR programme needs to be depends entirely on the size and complexity of the task which it is required to perform. If one is dealing with a large corporation, extended management structure, numerous key messages to be targeted at numerous publics, numerous potential threats to reputation and issues affecting perceptions which need to be addressed, then inevitably the programme will be similarly extensive and is likely to require a great deal of activity, comparatively large budgets and very disciplined control systems. On the other hand a PR programme may be aimed at the single objective of successfully reaching a single defined target audience with a single key message and may, therefore, be very straight-forward.

But no matter how complex or simple the programme is, it will always work vastly more effectively if it is planned through in the way described. It is the logic of what one is doing and the need to focus activity which demands a formal structure, not the complexity. Even if the key stages can be adequately set out on the back of an envelope, the process of thinking through the steps listed above is always worth doing.

There is, however, a paradox in all this talk of formal approach and that is that one needs to be flexible in running a PR operation. Opportunistic PR can often be extremely effective and any approach which is so rigid that it doesn't allow for any action other than that listed formally in the programme will inhibit taking advantage of such opportunities. Equally impor-tantly, circumstances change all the time and nowhere faster than in terms of perceptions. So an effective programme must be able to change with changed circumstances and must be flexible enough to be modified on a running basis.

Typically a rapidly changing set of circumstances occurs when one is dealing with defensive PR operations, for example an attack on one's products brought about by ill informed or mis-understood comment from an apparently reliable source such as the problems caused to the British egg industry by Edwina Currie's comments on listeria. What tends to happen in these circumstances is that there is a constant development of events which means that perceptions are changing at a rapid pace and so are the concerns and interests of one's target public.

These changing circumstances will also occur, though usually less dramatically, during the normal operation of a PR cam-paign and may change due to circumstances which appear to

38

have no direct bearing on the immediate aims and objectives of one's PR programme. Thus changes in the public attitude to 'green' issues will have an implication for what aspects of a company or its products are of most interest, or changes in legislation may have a direct impact on attitudes towards particular products, or any one of a host of events or fashions changes may mean that one needs to modify key messages or identify fresh target audiences.

The consequences of one's own PR efforts will also be to bring about changes in perception and a consequent need to modify one's approach in order to build on achievement.

Whatever the changing circumstances it is important that one's efforts towards creating 'mutual understanding and goodwill' should take them into account and this means that there is a need to monitor attitudes and awareness on a continuous basis. Since the very foundation of the PR programme depended in part on an assessment of prevailing attitudes it follows that changes in attitudes will lead to modifications in the programme.

So the paradox can be clearly seen. Unless one sets out a formal structure for any PR programme then that programme is likely to be ineffective particularly because PR activity readily admits muddled thinking, confused priorities and sloppiness of execution without a disciplined approach. Any PR programme which is determined too rigidly is likely to be ineffective because it will not allow for opportunistic action and because it will not take into account changing attitudes and a consequent need to modify objectives, messages and actions.

There is no absolute solution to this dilemma, but then again it is not such a serious problem provided one approaches it with a degree of common sense. Once one has established a formal approach and eliminated muddled thinking and sloppy execution from the PR programme, then a degree of flexibility can very readily be allowed, and is, indeed, essential. But the formal approach must be established first, otherwise there is little possibility that activity approached on a 'catch-as-catch-can'

39

basis, no matter how clever in execution or original in concept, will succeed in addressing itself to the proper targets and important issues.

This somewhat pompous and schoolmasterish discussion of the structure of a PR programme is not meant to inhibit good ideas, 'creativity' if you will, or enthusiasm, both of which are vital to a really effective operation. However, the very fact that PR can be such tremendous fun and can, on occasion, produce such startlingly effective results carries the very real danger that PR becomes seen as an end in itself. When this happens an air of self-congratulation is all too easily created and the only measure of effectiveness taken is a self-referring one – by this I mean that one starts to judge PR management simply by the standards of PR itself and not in a wider context of its benefit to the organisation as a whole.

40

PR is not an end in itself. For example, a successful press conference is not one where lots of journalists turn up and write lots of column inches. It is one where an organisation successfully co-operates with the media to disseminate well chosen messages to relevant audiences. This may indeed involve lots of journalists and lots of column inches but it is in the changed perceptions of the target audiences rather than in the mechanical success of PR techniques that the real success lies.

7

Media relations

For a great number of people who do not have any direct contact with public relations in practice the term 'PR' is synonymous with 'press relations', or, since one must recognise the ever-growing importance of radio and television, 'media relations'.

From Tony Curtis' wonderfully sleazy performance as a theatrical press agent in the film *The Sweet Smell of Success* to Jennifer Saunders' splendid portrayal of a deeply disturbed head of a PR consultancy in the TV series *Absolutely Fabulous*, 'PR' has been firmly identified with 'getting something in the papers' together with a high level of alcoholic entertaining – usually with the two intimately connected.

Not surprisingly PR people have fought long and hard to combat this image, and rightly so since it is grossly unfair. In doing so they have also tended to play down the importance of media relations within a PR programme in favour of elements such as 'strategic objectives', 'corporate positioning', 'issue management' etc, which have been touched on in the preceding chapter. One suspects that the motives for doing this have been mixed – some laudable and some rather more dubious.

It's perhaps worth looking briefly at what some of these motives may be.

The days when the majority of PR practitioners were drawn from the ranks of ex-journalists, and the ability to understand and service the press was the pre-eminent requirement for a PRO, have long passed and skill levels in media relations among PR 'professionals' have probably declined over the years. Nobody is likely to emphasise the value of skills which they don't possess.

Media relations activity is easy to understand and does not, therefore, carry the same 'consultative' or 'professional' clout as other aspects of the PR business. This means it is an activity less likely to enhance the status of the in-house operator and it is an activity less likely to command a high hourly fee rate for the consultant.

Because it is an activity which depends on third parties (the media) it is not fully controllable and results cannot be guaranteed in any way.

Simply because media relations is such a high profile and obvious aspect of PR it is often necessary to consciously push it temporarily to the background of one's thoughts when considering a PR programme for fear of missing other, less obvious but equally important, opportunities.

Media relations is a means to an end, not an end in itself. Pursuit of media coverage for its own sake and outside the context of thought out aims and messages can be more damaging than useful despite a superficial impression of successful promotional activity.

These are just some of the likely reasons for 'professional' discussion of PR to give limited attention to the importance of dealing with the media. Don't be fooled, however. What people say and what actually happens are likely to be two different things.

Media relations remains the bedrock of most PR work and still accounts for at least half of the activity lumped together under the general title of 'PR'. Far more frequently than not, media relations, in one form or another, will be the single largest part of any PR programme. It is certainly likely to be the element in a programme in which success in achieving one's aims can be most accurately measured (see previous chapter) and is the aspect of PR work which reaches the widest, if not the most carefully selected, audience.

A large number of highly competent public relations operatives do nothing other than carry out press relations work and, certainly at the 'do-it-yourself' level, a PR programme which consists of media relations work and nothing else can be very effective. This is particularly true where PR is being used exclusively as a marketing support activity. It should be said, however, that it will almost certainly be the case that a programme confined to media relations alone, however good, would be even more effective if it included additional activities from the PR 'tool bag'.

Just as 'public relations' is a term which encompasses a range of activities so too does the term 'media relations' cover the use of a range of separate and distinct skills and techniques. Just as the range of PR activities are related in 'establishing and maintaining mutual understanding .. ', so too the apparently disparate techniques of media relations are all based on the same underlying principles.

43

The ability to negotiate the placement of a by-lined feature article in a specialist trade magazine has, on the surface, little connection with being able to provide a strong photo-news opportunity with appropriate 'sound bites' for coverage in a television news programme. Providing a range of clothes for a fashion shoot at a women's interest magazine seems a far cry from arranging a press and analysts' briefing to talk about the interim results of a quoted company. It would be possible to produce a very long list indeed of contrasting examples of media relations in action, but it is not the differences which should be of interest. It is the underlying similarities of approach common to virtually all successful media relations work which are important and which, once they are taken on board, should ensure that you can't go too far wrong.

The starting point for any media relations work is to recognise that the media has its own needs and that doing you a favour is not one of them. The media, from trade journal to national TV programme, will use information which you provide to them because they want to and not because you want them to.

So the first, and perhaps only, rule is to put yourself in the position of the journalist who will be considering your news story, feature article or whatever and considering whether what you have to say has any interest from his or her point of view. There will always be information which is of great interest to one publication or programme but which is not even marginally relevant to others. (Nothing is gained by wasting people's time through sending irrelevant information; indeed harm may be done for the future when you *do* have something which is of interest.)

Often it's not simply a question of whether or not a story is of interest but rather one of whether or not an item of information can be made of interest. You need to consider how you can tailor the information which you want to provide so that it matches the interests of the medium to which you are giving it. Provided there is some commonality of interest between the information which you want to disseminate and the information which a particular medium habitually carries then it should be perfectly possible to tailor what you have to say to make it both relevant and interesting. But you can only do this if you put yourself in the journalist's shoes first.

It's also worth remembering that journalists are people as well as members of the Fourth Estate. They have their own needs, pressures and jobs to do. This means that the easier you make it for them to do their job then the more likely you are to succeed in getting them to carry your information in a form which at least approximates to the way you would like to see it. This goes a lot further than the questions of content and emphasis which we've just looked at. It covers the simple mechanics of life – getting information there in time for deadlines, making sure that a TV crew has something to point its camera at to illustrate the story, making life easy for the sub-editors by providing copy in a manageable form etc.

Much of the time media relations work is concerned with attempting to disseminate information which has genuine value, and which you want to be carried as widely and in as much depth as possible, but which is not an automatic front page story. How fully your information is used, what slant is put on it by the media, even whether it is used at all, will depend almost entirely on how successful you have been in understanding the media's needs and interests in the first place.

The apparent contrasts in the examples of different types of media relations work which were given as illustrations above result directly from the fact that the requirements and interests of the different bits of the media involved are themselves very different. The difference in the actions of anybody carrying out media relations work to meet these requirements is a reflection of the recognition of these needs because this is what media relations amounts to – helping the media so that the media will help you.

To some extent this fundamental requirement of good media relations – seeing things from the media's point of view – can only be fully achieved through experience and through taking time and trouble to get to know the particular sectors of the media which are likely to be of direct importance to you. It really is worth taking some care to consider the style and content of key publications and programmes, and to get to know specific key journalists with whom you are likely to have regular contact – dialogue at this level can be mutually beneficial, providing the journalist with a reliable information source which understands his needs and interests and providing you with ready access to a key channel for distributing information.

45

You don't need to have spent years on Fleet Street, however, nor to have spent years working in PR, to be able to understand some of the basic needs of the media. There are a number of fairly simple rules to follow which will take you a large part of the way and there is a great deal of readily available reference material which can provide you with key background information.

The next few short chapters deal with specific aspects of media relations work and attempt to set out the basic rules which should be followed. This approach is adopted to try to present the information in a digestible form rather than have a huge, rambling discussion of media relations contained in one extended chapter. Hopefully this will make for ease of reference if required and ease of understanding by breaking down a mass of primarily factual information and best practice rules into a series of bite size chunks.

A word of warning is, however, in order. Although separate chapters cover the main media relations activities those activities are normally not, themselves, so separate. One single event may well cut across a number of activities. For example, holding a press conference does not mean that you don't also have to issue a news release, consider the needs of the broadcast media as distinct from printed publications, possibly set up some one to one press meetings in addition and, maybe, negotiate follow up feature articles. You may bring particular efforts to bear to handle some particular activity within a media relations programme but if you lose sight of the programme as a whole you will inevitably finish up missing out on opportunities.

Any or all of the activities talked about may be relevant to a particular media relations programme. What you do and how it is done will always be determined by particular situations but successful media relations will always depend on following the simple yardstick that the media is made up of individuals all with their own agenda, their own needs and their own interests. Insofar as you are able to help them they will prove to be your allies and help you with the job of disseminating information but they owe you nothing and have no obligation to do what you want.

If you expect members of the media to carry advertising copy as editorial, if you expect them to suppress information because it is inconvenient to you, if you expect to be able to bully them, if you expect them to put your interests before the requirements of their job, then you're likely to be disappointed. On the other hand if you take trouble to give them what they want and in the form they want it, if you take time to understand their needs, if you work on developing relationships with key contacts, then you might be surprised at how helpful and supportive the media can be.

8

News releases

The news release or press release is the fundamental weapon of media relations work. It is a basic working tool and, as such, is all too often treated with far less respect than it deserves.

'Any fool can write a press release,' thinks the same company chairman who will agonise for hours over the contents of a speech to the local branch of Rotary. 'Press releases are handled by our (junior) writing staff,' says the PR consultant who is probably charging £100 plus an hour for choosing the wine to be served at a press lunch. 'We'll just take the copy from the sales leaflet,' says the publicity manager who's just spent a week writing a slide presentation on promotional support for the monthly sales meeting.

If you're not prepared to recognise that what you write in a press release, how you write it, how you present it and who you send it to deserves serious thought and careful planning then the chances are that your media relations programme is doomed before it's even started.

The media relies heavily on information provided to it by third parties carrying out some form of media relations activity, usually in the form of press releases. Taken across the printed media of all types in the UK estimates of PR driven coverage range as high as 80 per cent. Yet it is reckoned that, on average, less than 20 per cent of press releases received by a publication are used in any form at all (for the national press and broadcast media the level of rejection is far higher), and that most of what is used appears in a significantly curtailed form.

It's very clear that the media needs press releases and that the opportunity to generate coverage for a product or a company is a real one. It's equally clear that there is a lot of competition out there and if you expect your release to be one of the less than one in five which see the light of day then you can't afford to leave it entirely to chance.

If you send advertising copy masquerading as news then the chances are it will be binned. If you send a release to arrive just after the copy deadline then the chances are it won't be considered. If you bury the news story somewhere in the middle of the release then the chances are that the editor receiving it won't persist long enough to find out what the story is. If your release is hard to read and hard to sub-edit then it won't be used unless it contains information of earth shattering importance. If a journalist has no way of getting back to you to fill in any gaps in the story then he'll probably choose to write about something else where full information is readily available. If you keep bombarding a journalist with press releases which are of absolutely no interest to him then by the time you send him something which he might want to use he's probably stopped reading anything which comes from you.

There are lots of ways in which it is easy to get it wrong when it comes to news releases and there are limited ways in which to get it right. The starting point is to ensure that any news release which is issued has at least got a chance to be given consideration by the publication or programme to which it is sent. Following a set of rules will not be a substitute for newsworthy content but at least it puts your news story in there with a chance. (The demands of broadcast media are revisited in a later chapter since there tend to be additional considerations for this sector of the media.)

Basic rules for news releases

SEND IT TO THE RIGHT PEOPLE

It's a massive waste of time and effort to mail out news releases to publications or programmes which have no interest in them or to the wrong people on the right publication. Working out a basic distribution list is relatively straightforward since there are a number of directories which provide details of publications, names of specialist writers and all the mechanical data which you are likely to need – addresses, telephone numbers, frequency of publication, copy deadlines etc. These lists are also regularly updated since people in the media move around quite as much as in any other industry and publications also come and go with some frequency. They will also handle the physical distribution of releases either in hard copy or electronic form should you wish (see Chapter 26 for contact names and addresses).

Of course, no reference work, however detailed, is a substitute for direct knowledge and it is very worthwhile building up one's own press distribution lists covering known key publications and key journalists, including a directory of freelance writers who may not be so easily contactable through standard directories.

49

If a press release is going to work well for you then you need to make sure that all, and only, those sectors of the media who might wish to use it have access to it. Time spent on getting press lists right at the start, tailoring the list to each particular press release and ensuring that lists are kept up to date is, invariably, time well spent.

GET IT THERE AT THE RIGHT TIME

Timing is all important when you're dealing with news items and journalists work to deadlines. If you ignore their deadlines, whether they be weeks ahead for a monthly magazine or hours ahead for a television newscast, then they will ignore your news story.

MAKE IT EASY TO READ AND SUB-EDIT

All things being equal, a journalist is always going to prefer to use a news release which he can work with easily to one which causes him problems. This can be a matter of physical present- ation as well as a matter of content. So it makes sense to get the simple rules of presentation right:

- always provide press releases double-spaced, on one side of the paper only and with good, wide margins. As well as making it easier to read and absorb the contents quickly this makes sub-editing or re-writing much easier for an editor, journalist or sub

- use standard press style for copy, again to make life easier for the journalist. There are a number of press conventions which are too numerous to go into in detail here, and which don't need to be followed to the ultimate detail. However it is worth being aware and following the main, and universally adopted conventions of which the following are a few examples:

  - numbers up to ten should be written and from 11 upwards shown as numerals
  - dates should be shown without suffixes, thus September 10 not 10th September
  - never use unnecessary capital letters even for titles
  - the first time you use an acronym spell it out in full and bracket the initials, thereafter you may shorten, thus 'United Nations (UN)' on first occurrence in the text, followed by 'UN' on sub-sequent occurrences
  - don't underline: this is a print direction for italics.

- always ensure that there is a contact address and telephone number on the bottom of the release for further information. (If you've done this there is absolutely no reason to pester a journalist by ringing up after sending the release to 'see if you've got it safely and can I give you any more information', a tactic quite likely to result in the story being spiked imme- diately)

- make sure that the release is clearly dated – journalists need to know that what they are reading is not last week's news.

REMEMBER IT'S A NEWS STORY NOT A BROCHURE

If the physical presentation of a news release is important then so too is the way in which the contents are written. A news release is just what it says it is – a release of information which is newsworthy. If the recipient cannot recognise news value quickly and easily then he's not going to take it seriously so one needs to follow the basic rules of press reporting.

- tell the story clearly in the first couple of paragraphs and don't bury it in the body of the release
- Present information factually; don't 'editorialise' or present promotional copy as if it is news but stick to factual information. (If you want to bring in opinion then you may legitimately do this as attributed quotes – normally towards the end of the release)
- Structure the story so that information of decreasing importance is carried in the latter part of the release. This is an extension of the basic rule of telling the main story in the first two paragraphs and, when done properly, enables the release to be 'subbed' from the bottom up, thus making it easy for a journalist to cut the story to length when he has a specific area to fill.

51

None of this will make an essentially non newsworthy release more newsworthy but it will put it into the context of a genuine piece of copy for consideration and not a promotional 'puff' to be rejected if possible. Sometimes one reads editorial which is quite clearly advertising copy masquerading as editorial but, by and large, there is nothing which a journalist dislikes more than the blatant attempt to gain editorial coverage for promotional material without editorial merit.

REMEMBER WHO YOU'RE TALKING TO

Presentation and style are vital but there is no substitute for producing genuinely newsworthy material which meets the editorial needs of the publications you're aiming at. Just because something seems tremendously important to you does not mean that it is automatically of interest to the people you would like to tell about it or to the media which you expect to use as an information channel. Just because a story is of interest to one sector of your target media it does not follow that it is equally interesting to all sectors or that the 'slant' which will be put on the story will be common to all. It can also be the case that something which you do not see as being critically important is of very considerable interest beyond the boundaries of your organisation.

If you expect news releases to be picked up then you need to make sure that their essential content is usable. This means you need to understand what it is that your target press needs and to present information in a way that meets these needs. One only has to consider the various ways and various different emphases which may be placed on a news story by the national press to see how interests vary. The national press is a relatively homogenous body and there will be a fair degree of unanimity about what does and doesn't constitute a genuinely important news item, so one doesn't need too much imagination to realise how disparate may be the interests of the media as a whole ranging, as it does, across a vast range of consumer magazines, local and provincial press, commercial trade press, technical trade press, special interest magazines, business publications etc, and with a similarly wide and ever expanding broadcast media at local, national and international level.

If a press release is really going to work it is not enough for it to contain a germ of newsworthy material it must also contain that material written in a way which will appeal to the recipients.

This is, unfortunately, not an area where it is possible to lay down a series of rules which, if faithfully followed, will guarantee a relevant and useable news release. It is a combination of experience, 'feel' and flair which will result in the press release which captures the attention, wins coverage and provides you with a vehicle for getting key messages across to your target public. The only real guideline is the fundamental one for

52

all media relations work which is to put yourself in the other chap's shoes – easier said than done but essential if one is to be a really effective user of media relations.

There are news stories of such clear importance that they are virtually guaranteed full and thorough coverage. There are occasions when it is possible to spin a news story almost out of thin air (some examples of how this has been done are included in Chapter 25). Generally, however, one is concerned to influence the tone and extent of coverage given to stories which are of legitimate interest but which may or may not be treated with the degree of respect which you undoubtedly believe that they deserve.

To have any real chance of this happening one needs to take the business of issuing news stories seriously. One needs to work hard at understanding what it is that interests one's particular key media and how that interest can be met. One needs to take time and trouble to identify the key news points in what one wishes to say – producing different releases with different news slants for different sectors of the media if necessary. One needs to present one's information in a way which is easy to absorb and easy to handle. One needs to accept that one is going to have failures as well as successes with press releases and that building a campaign is a matter of a continuing and planned programme rather than a once in a while, ad hoc activity.

Once one is prepared to take all of this on board, then it shouldn't take long before one realises what an extremely powerful and effective public relations tool the humble news release really is.

9

Press conferences, press briefings and photo calls

The first reaction which seems to occur to the tyro PR operator presented with a news story which a company's management wants publicising is liable to be 'let's hold a press conference'. It may be the appropriate response to a situation but very often it isn't. Press conferences are, or should be, serious business, demanding of time and preparation on the part of whoever holds them and demanding of precious writing time from the journalists who attend them. They're potentially fraught with danger and if you're going to hold one you shouldn't assume that it will be all plain sailing. When there's a doubt about whether or not one should call a press conference without there being a clear demand from the media or an obviously appropriate reason the best advice is usually 'don't'.

After press releases, press conferences are the most immediately thought of media relations activity and they most certainly do have a part to play in media relations. Before leaping cheerfully into setting up such events, however, let's consider just what's involved and just what the purpose of press conferences is.

Essentially, the prime justification for a press conference is that one is handling a news situation where the needs of the media can only be properly satisfied by a dialogue between journalists and the source of the news story. If the weight of media interest, sheer size of the story, urgency of the situation or complexity of the issues involved justifies setting up dialogue in this way then the press conference is an appropriate method for dealing with media interest.

Fast developing news stories demand a press conference approach. Stories which will clearly need a number of follow up questions from the press will normally require a press conference. Sometimes the media itself will demand the chance to ask questions and, by and large, such demands should be met. However, if a press conference is called simply to give a spurious added importance to an event which could as easily be handled in some other way then the result can be embarrassing all round and more damaging than helpful.

We need to look at the press conference as an aspect of media relations and we need to treat it very seriously but, in this same chapter, we should look at some alternative activities which, in some circumstances, may provide the PR operator with a more effective way of achieving his or her aims and not carry the downside of risking relationships with the media unnecessarily.

55

There are two distinct circumstances in which one may find oneself calling a press conference:

- one knows in advance that one has a major story to tell and one knows when this is going to happen
- events move at a fast and furious pace and the sensible way to deal with media pressure is to call a conference and deal directly with their queries.

The rules for both circumstances are much the same, but in the second instance may prove rather more difficult to follow. No attempt to set down guidelines can hope to deal with all the circumstances which one may run into but it is, perhaps, helpful to set down a number of indications of actions which one is well advised to take:

- ensure that the conference has a clear structure so that questions and answers can be dealt with in an orderly way. This normally entails having a chairperson who is not the main spokesperson and whose role is one of management and control

- make sure the spokesperson is speaking from a prepared text as far as possible and does not attempt to 'wing it'. This is live media contact and there are no opportunities for retakes

- try to anticipate likely questions and have responses prepared for these (you can't expect the main spokesperson to have all the facts and figures at his or her fingertips so make sure these are readily to hand)

- prepare as much information as possible in written form and provide it to the media in writing, following the simple rules for news releases discussed in the previous chapter. Journalists are human and make mistakes, forget things or misunderstand just like anyone else and written text minimises this

- if possible ensure the timing of the conference is convenient to the media and fits in with their deadlines. This may entail deciding which of the likely attendees is of most importance and gearing timing to their needs – evening press coverage can damage the next day's reporting although evening TV has little effect, for example

- take some trouble over choosing the location for the conference and remember it is the media's convenience, not that of your company chairman which is important in making this choice

- never, never, get clever in a press conference by going 'off the record', assuming that the media know when you're joking rather than giving a serious response, or speaking before thinking

- do make sure that you have covered everyone in issuing invitations and get these out in good time – it is perfectly acceptable, indeed essential, to ring round as a reminder and check on attendance; the media is forgetful, bad at responding and prone to take last-minute decisions on what events to cover

- Don't forget TV and radio may have special requirements in terms of lighting and power and may want opportunities for interviews outside the conference

- if you have the opportunity then 'dress' the conference set to get maximum benefit from TV and photographic coverage of the event
- do recognise that a press conference is a first-rate opportunity to establish useful contact with the media and, particularly for conferences prepared well in advance, plan to use the occasion to set up future, follow-up activities with key press.

Mostly the type of press conference which one is considering, particularly where PR is operating as part of the marketing mix, will not be a high pressure event of the sort characterised by crisis management and there will be the opportunity to prepare well in advance. It's worth making full use of this preparation time and having rehearsals if possible. At the end of the day, however, it is probably better not to be too slick in presentation and it is important to remember that this is a media event and not a sales conference – all of the caveats which apply to press releases apply even more strongly to the press conference.

57

These few guidelines won't ensure that you have a successful conference but they may help to avoid the most obvious pitfalls and give you a fair chance of running a successful event. A good press conference can be one of the most satisfying activities for a PR operative to carry out and it can be a rapid and effective method of communicating one's message widely and rapidly.

Just because you feel that what you have to say deserves more than simply sending out a press release doesn't mean that you have to move to running a press conference and it's well worth considering some of the other ways in which a story can be given a little extra weight without the heavy cost and attendant dangers of a full-scale press conference.

Later in this book we'll talk about the value of photography within a PR programme and, in the present context, a photocall can provide just that extra lift to a story which one might hope to get from a press conference but where such a conference is not really justifiable. Of course a photocall is only justifiable if you can provide a good strong picture element to your story and here a degree of creativity is called for – indeed sufficient creativity will generate a strong story where none really exists simply through providing a good picture. Celebrities are usually one possibility, if not particularly imaginative; so too, in our determinedly sexist society, are pictures involving pretty women, but with a little imagination one should be able to identify various other possibilities (some ideas which have worked really well are mentioned in Chapter 25).

Whatever you select as a photo opportunity if it provides a good picture you will have achieved much the same result as may have been hoped for from a press conference and rather more simply and at less risk. It is much easier to get a photographer to attend an event of marginal interest than to get a journalist, and much less of his or her time is involved so the odds on a decent turn-out are much better. In precisely the same way as you can be reasonably sure that a journalist attending a press conference needs to justify his time by filing copy, so too a photographer will submit prints for publication. Careful co-ordination should mean that you file your news story in parallel with the photo call, giving you two bites of the editorial cherry. Best of all you have not wasted any editorial time and pre-judiced your chances of a successful press conference when the genuinely strong story comes around.

You might also consider the press briefing approach as an alternative to a full press conference, particularly where the story you have to tell is relatively specialist in nature, for example technical product or service launches, narrow based industry investment programme. The advantage of the press briefing, either held as a series of one to ones or as a small specialist group, is that you provide the same opportunities for dialogue to those members of the media who are really interested without the need to pack the conference with other journalists whose interest may only be peripheral and whose only real interest is in what refreshments are on offer. The press briefing approach does not preclude the issue of a press release to non-core press – probably generating as much interest as a poor conference among fringe press – but allows your key media contacts to feel that they have the story in depth and on a semi exclusive basis which encourages greater treatment in depth.

The so-called 'facility visit', sometimes more accurately described as a press junket, also avoids the more obvious dangers of a press conference. Facility visits can cover everything from a site visit to the Midlands in order to see a new ball bearing production line to an exotic trip to a Cayman island resort hotel in order to have details of a new tax effective personal savings scheme explained. They have, in common, that the demand made on media time does not pretend to be justified entirely by the flat facts of the story which one has to tell. By the very fact of asking for a longer time commitment from the media than would be necessary just to tell them what the news is one is offering something a little more. What that little more is depends very much on the particular event. Certainly it contains elements of hospitality and entertainment but it also offers the chance for a subject to be looked at in depth, with the chance for a journalist to fill in the background to the information received and usually with the potential for full feature, rather than simply news, coverage to result from the event.

Within reason journalists quite like this sort of approach and appreciate time and trouble taken over them. This is not to say that they are the load of free loaders of the type popularised in the pages of fiction and in the movies. Lashings of champagne do not provide a sufficient reason for wasting people's time but if a good story can be combined with a chance to garner some additional information and can be enjoyable into the bargain then that's normally fine. After all, a journalist can always turn you down with no harm done on either side, the only real crime is not delivering a story once you get to the ball-bearing plant or the Cayman Islands or wherever.

Press conferences, photo opportunities, press briefings, facility trips; they all add a dimension to media relations beyond that provided by the simple issue of press releases. They demand

59

more from the media than simply subbing a news story and that means that they need to offer more. They also carry a rather greater element of risk, not just for the PR programme but for the PR man himself – there can be few more nerve-racking moments than waiting in a fully dressed press conference room with no-one there but your company chairman, your marketing director and you 10 minutes after a press conference was due to begin.

10

Feature articles

Feature articles give one the opportunity to develop an idea or a body of information in depth. They don't have the same immediacy as a news story and they can't be placed across the media on a scattergun basis. They have to be organised on a one-by-one basis and each article may demand considerable input of PR time. In the right publication the impact of a good feature article can be worth the effort involved many times over. Unlike a news item it is also likely that a feature will have an extended life span through being kept for reference, both by interested readers and as a library source. Reprints of the article can be obtained from the publication and used as part of an organisation's continuing communications programme as giveaways, promotional literature or direct mail shots – the implicit third party endorsement of the information contained making this a very powerful form of sales literature. One should be prepared to devote serious effort to this aspect of media relations and recognise its value as a general marketing communications technique.

Feature articles come in two basic forms – the by-lined feature provided by a named individual from an organisation and identified as such and the feature written by a journalist, covering the organisation or some aspect of its operation.

In the case of the company by-lined article the opportunity to talk directly about one's organisation may be more limited, but control of precisely what is said lies in one's own hands. Although the by-line carried on such an article will normally be that of some authority figure within an organisation (the chairman or managing director, perhaps, or director responsible for the particular area of operation discussed in the article), the actual writing is more likely to be the responsibility of the PR function.

In the case of an article written by a journalist or a named contributor there may, ironically, be more direct 'puffery' about an organisation, but content is a matter of influence and provision of the raw information rather than of direct control. (Occasionally publications will accept articles written by PR people who are not credited as such and the article is presented as if written by the publication's own staff. This is relatively rare for publications of any real weight. More frequently publications will accept articles from a named contributor writing as a third party but, in fact, commissioned and paid by the organisation placing the article – a technique frequently used for syndicated articles – see below.)

As with all press relations work the starting point for running a feature article programme is to identify who, within your areas of target publications, wants what, and then set out to supply that need. Since features are placed on a one-to-one basis and since feature coverage is much more individual from publication than is general news coverage, there is usually a very definite need to match one's approach to a publication.

This means that a proper effort must be made to identify a publication's needs and preferences. Does the target publication have regular feature slots and, if so, what sort of subject areas do these cover? Does it run supplements on particular subjects made up of a number of features and, if so, what has it got planned for the future which fits with your own area of knowledge? Does the publication take by-lined pieces from outside contributors? What sort of length appears to be preferred for feature articles? How heavily are features supported by photographs or other illustrations? These are the types of questions which need to be addressed as a preliminary to attempting to place material on a one-to-one basis.

This is information which can only be obtained by looking at the target publications themselves and, over a period, analysing their contents. Additional information about planned forward features or special supplements can also be gained from a publication's advertisement department since such forward supplements are invariably tied in to an advertising push and from the publication 'Advance' (see Chapter 26) which provides just such information. (You need to know about forward plans of this sort to provide standard information and pictures and reference material to ensure your inclusion in many industry round-up supplements as part of your overall media relations programme, so the identification of future feature opportunities should not involve significant extra effort.)

Once you've decided on what sort of feature you want to place and with what publication it is a matter of agreeing this in principle with the editor or features editor. This doesn't have to be a long and complex process, carried out over extensive lunches! Assuming that the feature you have in mind is of interest and that an approach, by-lined article, staff writer or outside contributor, is easily agreed, there is no reason at all why an article can't be agreed in a simple telephone conversation or by an exchange of letters.

It is frequently a good idea to submit a brief synopsis of a proposed article for consideration and follow this up with a phone call; editors will often want to see a synopsis before agreeing to an article, particularly if they have not had much dealing with the writer. What you should not do is write an article on spec and then try to place it. Though I know circumstances can sometimes force this sort of approach it really is an amateurish way of going about things. Publications want articles tailored to their approach and may want the chance to modify a suggested article to meet their needs. Publications want to be able to specify length and may want to discuss who actually writes the article. The prepared article, offered on spec, meets none of these criteria and, even if provisionally accepted, stands a much greater chance of subsequent rejection than an article written specifically to an agreed brief.

Assuming reasonable common sense you won't sell an article which you can't deliver, but at the risk of stating the obvious here are a few things to remember before getting carried away by the thrill of negotiation with a target editor:

- make sure that you have all necessary permissions and clearances from any third parties who might be involved – this applies particularly to that favourite form of feature, the case history

- if you're offering a by-lined piece from within your organisation, make sure you've cleared writing and copy clearance procedures internally first (disagreement can mean delays and missed deadlines)

- make absolutely sure that you have access to the necessary information to deliver what you promise – there's a difference between a good outline idea and that idea properly researched and supported by evidence

- don't commit to supporting illustrations unless you know you've got them or can source them easily

- don't sell the idea of virtually the same article to rival publications without their knowing; you may get away with it once, but you'll be lucky to place any editorial with either of them again.

Assuming that you've looked at these basic points, the actual writing of a feature article suitable for publication should be a straightforward, if somewhat time-consuming, task. Stick to the agreed brief and bear in mind the tone and approach of the publication involved and you really shouldn't go too far wrong. However, if in doubt about your own ability to produce a worthwhile article, don't hesitate to buy in writing skill. There are plenty of freelance writers, and journalists who moonlight, who can be used and who are not over-expensive. Most self-respecting PR people are perfectly competent to write a feature article but, for a particularly important feature (in a special supplement in a quality national newspaper, for example) you might want to provide a little extra protection against being 'spiked' at the last minute because of poor final execution after all the work put in to negotiate the placement of an article.

When it comes to producing syndicated articles you may very

well want to use the specialist skills of a professional journalist and you may even want to commission a 'name' writer whose by-line can be used with the article. The syndicated article is normally quite different to the agreed placement, negotiated on a one-to-one basis. This type of article is usually written in advance and is then offered on spec to a number of publications. Obviously the papers to whom it is sent will normally be ones which do not compete with each other because of geographical or other differences of circulation. Thus syndicated features are offered to provincial and local newspapers, to regional chamber of commerce magazines, for use in company house journals etc.

As with a negotiated feature the initial approach will not usually involve sending the feature article itself but will be a matter of sending out a synopsis and inviting interest. The difference is that it is much more a 'take it or leave it' operation without further negotiation being entered into.

65

Areas in which syndicated features have proved to be particularly effective include home interests and home improvement, travel and holidays, gardening topics, personal finance, all offered on a geographically exclusive basis to the relevant specialist sections of regional press. This type of subject aimed at the consumer market has become standard fodder for syndicated articles but there is always room for more provided they can offer an interesting angle or approach. Business services too offer an opportunity for the syndicated article, particularly with the range of regional business publications which exist and even some of the standard features discussed above can have a second life as syndicated articles, copyright allowing, by re-offer internationally after suitable modification and translation where necessary.

Feature articles, whether written for a specific purpose or syndicated, add an additional dimension to press relations work of a type not provided by the news release and, although their immediate target is the same, they should not be thought of as being extended news releases. Just as we argued that a press release is not the place to editorialise but is about news, so the feature article is not the place to reveal news but is a place where one can speculate, explain, even indulge in a little reasonably camouflaged advertising copy.

The style and subject matter for features can be extremely varied and the approach and content for one publication may be very different from that adopted for another as, of course, will be the areas which different organisations may wish to cover. It's quite impossible to try to do more than indicate some of the possible approaches here, so no comprehensiveness is claimed for the following list which may, however, ring some bells or spark off some ideas:

- *the case history*, always of interest to technical publications and giving an opportunity for an organisation to demonstrate its service or product excellence by reference to real events

- *the issue or industry comment*, in the form of a by-lined article and, provided it is well-written and well-informed, enabling an organisation to appear to be taking the high ground and, implicitly, placing itself as a leading player

- *the interview*, arranged with a staff journalist, performs much the same role as industry or issue comment but with a rather less formal approach – also of great value where the interviewee is, himself, the product as with actors, pop stars, politicians and the like

- *the technical article*, providing genuine technical information on a subject which needs explaining, mainly confers benefit through the credit given to the by-lined author, though limited product reference may be possible

- *objective advice*, as a rule, is the approach adopted for a great number of syndicated articles as discussed above. Written from an apparently disinterested stance such articles actually enable the publicising of a particular viewpoint, product or range of services. This type of article may well be written about any subject you care to name but is most easily placed on the consumer front.

11

One-to-one press contact

When you're involved in media relations activity then, inevitably, you're involved with journalists and editors and, while some of this contact may be at arms' length, inevitably this must mean a fair degree of one-to-one contact. To state the obvious, building personal contacts and relationships with people in the media is important and there will be times when who you know really does matter as much as what you know.

Any press officer, with any level of competence, will have built up a string of journalist contacts and established relationships of mutual trust with a good number of these. It is part-and-parcel of the job.

Direct contact with the press will not be limited to the activities of a press officer, however, but will involve other members of an organisation on an occasional basis. Journalists value a good PR contact but there are times when they, and you, want the dialogue to be with the person who really knows, rather than with an intermediary – no matter how efficient, well-informed and helpful that intermediary may be.

Direct media contact is not limited to times of news stories or attempts to negotiate a particular feature article but is something which is worth pursuing in its own right in order to build a level of understanding which works on a continuing basis. With key journalists it should be the aim to ensure that when they receive anything from your organisation they treat it seriously and understand where it is coming from. More than this, it should become the case that you are regarded as a 'source' so that journalists will approach you for comment or information on subjects where your organisation may have something of value to say.

This kind of relationship takes time to build and can be fairly fragile. You're likely to be one of a large number of people who want to have an inside track to parts of the media and unless a regular contact is seen to be of mutual benefit, it will rapidly founder.

The fundamental starting point for building any kind of programme of one-to-one contact is to decide just who such a programme should involve. This will partly be determined by opportunity and fortuitous meetings, but mainly should be a matter of cool calculation. Work out which journalists are really important to you on a continuing basis and target them. Decide who should be introduced to other members of the organisation and on what basis. Take time to find out what particular subject areas are of particular interest and make sure that you are in a position to deliver in these areas.

The PR person who believes that there is no value in taking one's relationship with the press beyond maintaining accurate distribution lists for press releases, feature articles, captioned pictures and the like is wrong. The PR person who believes that the secret of press relations is simply to know and socialise with lots of journalists is equally wrong.

A profitable relationship with individual members of the press is one where both sides benefit and it is one which is normally defined by a number of unstated rules. These rules apply to one-to-one meetings and they also apply, though modified over time and by increased familiarity, to continuing regular contact.

Let's start by considering what both sides want from such contact. Journalists want to obtain news stories or feature material or, failing that, background information which deepens their knowledge of a sector about which they intend to write. PR people, or executives of organisations who are dealing with the press, want to place news items, or to provide specific background information which may be used at some time, or to influence an attitude by providing additional information, or to negotiate a feature article or, in some way, make use of the journalist's control of a channel of communication. These two separate sets of desires are mutually complementary in that each side wants something from the other. When that something turns out to be the same for both, then everybody's happy. So the first rule of one-to-one press contact is simple: *Make sure that any journalists or editors with whom you have contact benefit from the association.*

Simply because your interests and the interests of the media are not identical, there needs to be some degree of caution in dealing with difficult or sensitive issues. You cannot assume the goodwill and friendship of the press as a given, no matter how good you may feel the relationship is. Even the very best of the 'spin doctors' with their leaked information, unattributable quotes and 'off the record' comments have made the mistake of underestimating the extent of journalists' motivations to simply report news. *Never say anything which you are not prepared to have repeated.*

69

From this it directly follows that in conversations with journalists you don't guess, you don't speculate and you don't bluff. If you don't have the answer to a question to hand then say so and agree to discover the answer and let the journalist know. Then make sure that you keep your word. *Don't guess. Don't bluff. Don't lie. Don't speculate.*

There is a sub-text to these rules of total openness and this relates to comments made 'off the record' – essentially information which is given for background information but which will not be used by the journalist – and 'attributable' information which is provided in the understanding that it may be used but will not be attributed to any source. These are tricky techniques to employ and it is very easy to become over-clever but they can allow a dialogue of greater depth than one confined by excessive caution. *Never go 'off the record' or unattributable without clearly agreeing the status of the information exchange, in advance, with the journalist concerned.*

Journalists make mistakes, just like anyone else, and the same principle of providing written facts applies to one-to-one contact as to press conferences when it comes to avoiding unintentional errors of reporting. It also makes life easier for a journalist and allows a greater concentration on dialogue rather than just factual note taking. *Provide factual information in writing wherever possible.*

It's worth remembering that no one-to-one contact is conducted in a vacuum. Just as a journalist has many other contacts and information sources trying to get his ear, so too do you have other press contacts whom you wish to influence. You certainly make a contact beneficial for a journalist if you keep feeding him exclusives, but bear in mind what this may mean for the quality of other relationships with the media. Also remember that worthwhile press contacts last over time and price of any short term manipulation of a journalist (which can be achieved, journalists are no more omniscient than anyone else) may well carry a long-term cost. *Don't get carried away by present benefit in dealing with an individual journalist but remember the wider considerations.*

All person-to-person relationships are far more subtle than can be set down in a simple set of rules and, particularly when one is dealing with a longer-term contact, the dynamics of such relationships are almost infinitely variable. You shouldn't expect every contact with every journalist to yield benefit to you every time. You should be aware that favours done now may have long-term benefits and that favours received now may have to be paid for in the future. Provided you follow the first rule of remembering the need for mutual benefit, then the degree to which you build useful media contacts will depend very much on the normal social skills which we all employ all the time.

The fact that the few rules set out above are mainly prescriptive should not be allowed to make dealings with the press overly inhibited. As in all dealings between people the best starting point is a mutual liking and respect and the value of friendships should never be underestimated.

Both you and your media contacts have a business reason for talking, however, and nothing is likely to change that. This means that you must stay in control of your side of the information exchange. It's very easy to get carried away. So the last rule, not entirely tongue in cheek is yet one more prescription. *Don't get drunk, on alcohol, or adrenaline, or friendship, or even on your own cleverness.*

By and large, if you're fair with the media then the media will be fair with you. This applies in a general sense and it applies to individuals. It applies to one-off meetings and it applies to longer-term relationships. But it should never be taken for granted.

71

12

Broadcast media

A classic phrase in PR proposals from consultancies over the years when referring to radio and television has been 'These media must be viewed realistically'. It is PR shorthand for saying 'It's really hard to get significant coverage in the broadcast media unless you're an extremely high profile organisation, so we'll give it our best shot but don't have unrealistic expectations'.

The phrase, or some equivalent, appears less frequently these days, mainly due to the explosion in opportunities for coverage which has taken place with the changes in broadcasting over the years. It used to be the case that there was massive competition for very limited air time indeed and PR people were, quite rightly, fairly pessimistic about the chances of gaining coverage in such a tight environment. This has changed dramatically over the years with the development of greatly extended regional radio, BBC and commercial, with increased regional coverage from the Independent Television companies and with the advent of satellite television. There is a great deal more air time available and a far greater width of coverage within the broadcasting media.

One suspects that a second reason why PR people are less pessimistic about coverage on the air waves is that they have got a lot better at it, have a much clearer idea about what the needs of the broadcast media are likely to be and a better understanding of how to meet those needs.

In principle the needs of radio and television are not so very different from the rest of the media. In practice there is a whole series of considerations which determine the rightness of a story for TV or radio which just doesn't come into calculations for the press. Predominant among these are considerations of how a suggested item will work on the medium. An interview is stronger on radio than a simple news piece. A television piece with good visual content is always better than a non-visual story and, all things being equal, will be used in preference.

Deadlines are different too, and so is the need to plan ahead. A television news or magazine programme will not take final decisions on where to send its outside camera teams until the morning of the day of broadcast, but it will need information on the whats, whys and wherefores, of a possible story in advance, so for anything other than lead news items broadcasting media actually need more advance notice than newspapers, despite the fact that they appear more 'immediate' in their news coverage.

The short booklet produced by Two-Ten Communications entitled 'How to get into the media' gives a useful and perceptive description of the way in which news coverage may be sought on radio and television. Even allowing for the fact that Two-Ten have an axe to grind as the premiere PR support operation specialising in distribution of media material, including syndicated radio tapes and video news releases, the advice which they give in this extract is first rate and equally valid whether or not one uses their particular services.

73

> Radio and television newsrooms may produce audio and video output, but like newspapers and magazines they usually start from the written word.

> News editors and editorial departments receive and handle press releases in the same way that publishers do. At smaller radio stations there may be no news desk as such, in which case individual programme presenters should be contacted direct.

> National news coverage is generally centralised: at BBC radio and television in London, ITN (for all commercial TV news programmes), IRN and Network News (which supply feeds to almost all commercial radio stations) and Sky News. It is seldom worth sending a national story to individual stations and channels unless there is an obvious regional angle (e.g. where the national story is

about an invention of a technological breakthrough but the local angle may be on the person or factory which made it).

However, often the most effective way to get broadcast cover is to supply not the written word but audio or video material.

Radio

Local radio stations have for some years accepted radio tapes in the form of broadcast quality interviews with an expert, recorded in a studio with professional assistance. As you would expect, stations will use such tapes where the expert speaks with general appeal: a tape which mentions Brand X in every sentence will join that day's press releases in the bin!

Alternatively, your experts can be interviewed live by several stations in succession, using a studio such as the one at Two-Ten linked directly to each station in turn. Thus a spot on radio in Plymouth can be followed minutes later by one in Newcastle without the interviewee leaving their seat.

Television

The 1990s has seen increasing use of the video news release (VNR). As the phrase suggests, it is a press release on videotape; but what television stations require is very different from the needs of radio.

Ideally a VNR will contain around four minutes of footage, with a script which merely describes what is being shown. Usually, a further 20 minutes of more general footage, without script, is added at the end. On no account should you include a spoken soundtrack; your VNR will only be shown while the station's own reporter or presenter talks to their own script.

VNRs are increasingly used to provide footage of new products, processes, factories etc. Television is a visual medium. News stories of any length have to be accompanied by pictures. It is very difficult for a TV station to film your story and therefore your VNR will be much appreciated. Often, of course, a story which might have been of marginal news value – and thus the TV station did not send a crew to cover it, can get into the programme after all if the VNR is timely and visually interesting.

Of course it is not just news programmes which offer opportunities for broadcast exposure. There is a range of magazine, documentary, business, chat shows, and special interest programmes which may be of interest and relevance. Involvement in any such programmes can be discussed and negotiated in just the same way as with any part of the media – a letter to the producer followed up by a conversation and negotiation possibly leading to an agreement being reached. Producers are constantly on the look-out for relevant material to use and welcome such approaches provided they are relevant and sensibly conducted. One can imagine the number of ideas rejected for inclusion in a programme like *Tomorrow's World* and recognise the weight of suggestions received by the producer and research staff, but it is from these suggestions that the items which appear in the programme are drawn, so recognise that in putting forward a suggestion to a TV or radio programme one is not asking for a favour but is providing for a real need.

This assumes that what one is offering is a genuine 'runner' and you won't achieve this without doing some homework into what the needs of a programme may be – it's not likely to be sensible to offer a late night chat show the chance to talk to an expert in some specialist manufacturing process, but in some circumstances the same expert might be welcomed with open arms onto the money programme. (Incidentally, most current affairs and business programmes hold lists of experts that they can call on as the need arises and it can be worthwhile ensuring that appropriate company spokespeople are included in such lists.) Similarly drawing the attention of a holiday programme to an exotic new location may well be worthwhile but it's likely to be a waste of time approaching a general news programme with the same suggested item – even though both programmes might be broadly described as falling into the 'magazine' category. If this seems a bit obvious then a quick look through the typical post bag of broadcasting programmes will quickly reveal how little homework many supposed PR professionals are prepared to do. The same sort of research is required as has previously been discussed in relation to press relations. Programmes have different requirements. They have different preparation times, from a matter of hours to months in some cases. They have different approaches. All of this should be taken into account before approaching any programme.

75

It's easy enough to identify just what programmes exist through such reference books as the *Blue Book of British Broadcasting* and to select from these those which might be of interest. It takes a little more effort to acquaint oneself directly with programmes which might be of value but it is still not difficult. It takes a bit of time and trouble to gear your approach to a programme's identified needs, but again this is not hard. If one is serious about including radio and television as an integral part of any media relations programme, then there is no real excuse for not carrying out these simple steps.

Television and, to a slightly lesser extent, radio have a huge reach. A networked TV programme may have up to 20 million viewers and radio programmes such as the *Jimmy Young Show* have a larger audience for interviews and feature items than national newspapers. It is not surprising then that gaining broadcast coverage is sometimes seen as the Holy Grail of the PR industry. A word of caution is in order here, however. TV and appearances and radio interviews can go horribly wrong and ill prepared performances by company spokespeople who neither understand nor have been trained can do vastly more harm than good.

Professional training is available from a number of organisations and covers TV and radio appearances. For anyone who is likely to act as an organisation's spokesperson such training is a most sensible investment.

13

A picture is worth
a thousand words

We live in a world where visual information has become more and more important. The claim that a picture is worth a thousand words was probably something of an exaggeration when it was first made but it has become increasingly true as the population as a whole becomes more and more used to dealing with pictorial rather than written information. A number of studies have confirmed that, despite literacy levels remaining more or less steady, people rely less and less on the printed or spoken word as their sole information source.

The sheer dramatic impact of the pictures of famine in Africa or reports from various wars from Vietnam onwards underline just how powerfully visual coverage reinforces the spoken or written message and this is true of still photography as well as of film or video coverage.

Why there has been this increase in the power of visual images is open to debate, but one does not need to be an academic sociologist to make the reasonably informed guess that the influence of television and the quality of TV news presentation has something to do with it, or that improvements in printing techniques and consequent improvements in photo reproduction may have some relevance. It may even be that the growth computer and arcade games with their ever more sophisticated graphics exerts some influence. Whatever the reason for the increased impact of pictures as opposed to the written word, it is clear that the PR operator who ignores the opportunities for communication through pictures is likely to be missing a trick or two.

Money spent on good quality photography can be money spent intelligently and cost effectively and, with the ready availability of video, one's horizons should not be limited to the possibilities offered by static photography. At the same time it is very easy to pour money away on photography which is never used or which is of a quality which is inappropriate. This applies just as much to spending too little on pictures which will never get used as it does to investing in over-elaborate photo sessions.

There's nothing very complicated about the use of photography within a PR campaign – video is a little more complex and we'll leave discussion of it for the moment. Essentially all one needs to do is to be aware of the value of being able to show as well as to talk and to realise that this has relevance to virtually every aspect of PR which is discussed in this book.

78

At its most basic level, a photograph which accompanies a press release will give you a greater chance of gaining more coverage. Stories aren't cut to accommodate pictures as a general rule and a story which is supported by a reasonable picture is more likely to be used since publications are generally more in need of photographs than they are of news stories (we discussed earlier the large number of press releases which never see the light of day). It's also worth recognising that a photograph, suitably captioned, may well be used irrespective of its immediate news value since pictures are often treated more like feature material than news items, so a planned programme of picture release can lead to continued media presence even when there is an absence of news to hang press releases on.

At a more sophisticated level one should recognise that intelligently used photography can provide more information and more 'feel' for what you wish to express than is usually possible with words alone. This applies to your own print and publications, to exhibition displays, as support for slide presentations, in media relations and, indeed, right across the range of PR activity.

It can be very expensive to commission photography every time one thinks one has a need if one treats the whole business of pictures on an ad hoc basis and doesn't follow a planned policy. But if one plans one's approach then budgets don't have to be excessive. It costs money to employ a photographer but once you've paid for him to attend a photo session then it costs very little extra to make full use of his time. Every time you have a product shoot intended for advertising or sales brochure pictures make sure that you also shoot some film which provides pictures suitable for PR use. By the same token remember that once you've got your photographer it costs very little extra to shoot extra pictures in black and white as well as colour, and you may have a use for these at a cheaper print cost. Ensure that you build up a continuing photographic file and make use of it to draw on established shots as illustrations for feature articles or news stories. (Incidently one should always make sure that pictures sent to the media have a clear caption attached to them – pictures get separated from the news story or feature article which they illustrate in busy editorial offices and if they cannot be identified quickly and easily then they won't be used.)

79

Photography is a subject about which one can write volumes, covering aesthetic and technical considerations, but this is not the place for such a discussion. It is enough to point out that all pictures are not suitable for all applications and that a little time and effort ensuring that one has the pictures to meet the needs is time well spent. In terms of media relations work it's worth familiarising oneself with the sort of pictures which key publications prefer to use and matching what one submits to them to these preferences – this applies to subject matter and to technical considerations. Some publications can handle fine detail and colour variation whereas with others, such as newsprint, over-subtle shots will simply not reproduce well. There are preferences for the use of portrait or landscape formats in different sections of publications and these should be born in mind. Simply reading the publications will give some indication of editorial prejudices, such as the general preference of marketing and communications magazines for 'different' pictures over simple head-and-shoulders shots to accompany stories about people, or the *Financial Times'* apparent preference for hard contrast pictures in black and white, possibly because of a combination of newsprint production and a pink ground colour. (In fact the wheel seems to have swung full circle for some publications and black and white has become a rather fashionable alternative to colour photography provided it is of good quality.)

Where one controls the use of pictures more directly, as in PR activity which does not involve media relations or those grey areas between PR and promotion such as corporate advertising, annual reports etc, the use of pictures becomes a design consideration beyond the scope of this discussion. However, the fundamental consideration continues to apply that where there is a chance to show something visually it's usually worth taking.

80

The power of photography is considerable, or indeed of static graphics used to supplement the spoken word. With the development of video this power of pictures has increased to include movement and, unlike film, has become something which can be viably considered as a standard item within the PR operator's tool box.

There's absolutely no point in rushing out and using video techniques where they are not needed. Nothing, for example, is gained by putting material best suited to a slide presentation onto video just for the sake of it. But in areas where one might previously have felt oneself limited to the spoken or written word there are some real opportunities to use video really effectively.

The video press release is a relatively recent development which can work well, particularly where one has a good, strong story suitable for TV but where it might not be strong enough to demand the expensive time of outside broadcast crew attendance. The greatly increased number of TV stations, land-based and satellite, which are now potential placements of news items means that there are similarly increased possibilities for the use of the video release. As with any media release you need to make sure that what you issue is usable by them and, with video, there is limited opportunity for the sort of sub-editing or rewriting which can be carried through by the print media. This means your release must be useable as it stands – both from the point of view of content and in terms of technical quality. This really isn't something which you can consider doing yourself but requires expert support. You need to buy in the skills to structure and film a video release and this isn't particularly cheap but the good news is that the same people who produce your news story will also help you place it by ensuring distribution to the right potential users at the right time and in the right format. For the big story video release must always be a consideration.

Other areas where video may be seriously considered within a PR programme are:

- as an alternative to newsletters both internal and external;
- for standard corporate presentations, acting as a supplement to the normal corporate brochure approach;
- for specialist staff communications programmes, particularly in large companies or organisations operating from a number of separate sites.

For all such uses it is worth going to specialists for production – there's very little which looks worse than an amateur video. The cost is not prohibitive, and can be carefully controlled provided you make sure that you give a very clear brief to the production company and ensure that all the necessary logistics are sorted out on their behalf. Time-wasting through muddled or changing briefs and through lack of preparation are the reasons why video production runs over budget and these should be fully within your own control.

One last practical point to bear in mind about both photographic and video material, particularly when used in media relations is that, within reason, it's always worth making an effort to ensure that there is some clear branding element within the picture itself. You can't go over the top with this, since excessive branding turns a 'news' item into a publicity shot, but if there is an element of branding within a picture or video clip then it's not going to be edited out at the whim of a sub-editor, something which can never be guaranteed with the written word.

Both photography and video give you the opportunity to add an extra dimension to your communications activity and, while their use will not always be appropriate, they should always be kept in mind as possibilities when planning your PR programme. When opportunities exist, and budgets allow, a picture really can be worth a thousand words. It will certainly help boost your column inches of coverage, and will usually improve the quality of coverage as well as the quantity.

14

Exhibitions and speaker opportunities

Exhibitions usually cost a great deal of money. It's not just the investment which is made in the stand space, stand construction and stand fitting. It's the labour intensive nature of manning a stand and, frequently, the out-of-pocket expenses of stand staff staying and subsisting throughout the duration of the exhibition, to say nothing of the man hours spent on the fairly complex logistics of exhibition participation.

When one makes this kind of investment then it's important that the maximum benefit possible is extracted from the money spent. In the midst of the complications of arranging telephones on the stand, working out the manning roster, sending out complimentary tickets to actual and potential customers, flagging up trade advertising with 'See us on stand xyz at abc exhibition', fixing a trade reception during the show, fighting with the production side to make sure you've got the latest product available on the stand and all the myriad considerations which surround exhibition participation, it's easy to forget that a planned PR effort in support of exhibition participation is a virtually guaranteed way to capitalise further on your investment.

Participation at an exhibition provides a focal point on which to base a range of activities, including public relations work, but remember that this is equally true for all other exhibitors, who will normally include your direct competition.

For the purpose of discussing the PR input to exhibition partici-pation, let's assume that there is no need to deal with the mechanics of booking and building a stand, nor of dressing and manning the stand, nor of making sure your stand staff know what they're doing and have an efficient system for following up sales leads. Let's also assume that any support for your participation through advertising and through direct mailing customers and potential customers can be taken as read. What in addition can be expected of your PR function to maximise benefit from your participation?

The first and most obvious PR action is to take full advantage of the media relations opportunities which are standardly available through exhibition participation. These are relatively routine and it is surprising that all exhibitors do not take time to cover these basic actions, but they don't:

- any show worth its salt will have an exhibition press office. Make early contact with this and provide it with all the help and information you can. It is in their interest to gain coverage for the show and for its participants and they will welcome anything which you provide them with. (They may also be responsible for your catalogue entry but don't count on this and make sure you've checked thoroughly in your exhibitor's information pack.)

- get out a pre-show press release to all publications likely to carry an exhibition preview. Even quite weak stories will gain coverage in previews provided you meet their deadline. Product shots are always welcome.

- make sure you have provided sufficient, good press kits for use in the exhibition press office, clearly identifying your stand and a contact there, and have got them to the exhibition organisers well in time to be in the press room for press previews.

- try to mail out your main show press release within a day or two of the show opening. The chances are that not all your key journalists will attend and those that do may miss your press kit in the press room. (It will help you to build up a good press list for your show story and tell you who is interested in what if you can get a record of press coverage from the previous year's show. The show press office may well have a record of cuttings.)

- during the show visit the press office every two or three hours to check that your press kits and releases are available in the racks, and to pick up on any journalist contacts which you can make on the spot.

- press attending the show will have a lot to cover and a large number of people to meet. Nevertheless they are in attendance and an exhibition is a good time to arrange press meetings on the stand. Set these up in advance.

- unless you are a major organisation do not attempt to introduce new products to the press at a major show. They will simply get lost in the noise. Launch to potential customers by all means but, if you're looking for good media coverage, deal with the media outside the bustle of the show and out of the time frame of exhibition coverage. By the same token be very careful about holding a press conference during the show and, if you do, make absolutely certain it doesn't clash with any other major event or nobody will turn up.

These are the base rules and should be followed as an absolute minimum. If you're prepared to put in the effort then it may be that you can arrange to make your participation work harder still. Quite where PR ends and publicity begins at an exhibition is never quite clear and, anyway, it's a matter of purely academic interest. Some of the thoughts which follow may not strictly be regarded as PR, but they're worth considering and frequently finish up as the PR man's responsibility anyway.

Linked events

It's common practice for exhibitions, particularly in the technical field, to be linked to conference or seminar sessions. Participation in these as a speaker provides a double bite of the cherry and, using the text of any presentation made, a chance to increase exhibition-linked press coverage.

Speaker slots at such conferences are usually filled early, so it's worth making contact as soon as you consider exhibition participation.

The stand as a stage

Quite apart from making one's stand as attractive and eye-catching as possible you have the opportunity to use it as a base to stage events during the course of the exhibition. Collecting business cards through the day and holding a draw for some prize, champagne or whatever, creates a small stir around the stand and provides an easy way of tracking visitors to the stand. Indeed, most forms of competition run from the stand can be turned into an event which generates interest and coverage.

Happenings need not be limited to competitions. They may involve pre-arranged celebrity visits to the stand. They may involve a pre-arranged signing of a major order on the stand. They may involve tying-in events on the stand to happenings in the outside world (when a technical electronics exhibition coincided with the 25th anniversary of England's world cup win one enterprising exhibitor had England's hat trick striker Geoff Hurst running a special event from their stand). There are a number of possibilities and the limit is only the limit of your imagination.

Following up

After all the effort put into getting potential customers onto one's stand, it makes no sense at all to fail to follow up the leads gained. This happens all too often. The salesforce is inundated with leads over a very short period and can't cope without some back office support. Everyone goes into an exhausted, self-congratulatory slump at the end of an exhibition and follow-up gets put to one side.

Building in a proper system of follow-up which includes logging all enquiries (cards left in a goldfish bowl is really not adequate) and prioritising these for sales calls, issue of sales literature, telephone follow up etc is well worth doing. This involves a little specific training of the stand staff and establishing a back-up system to handle the secretarial elements of the job, which takes time and trouble but is greatly preferable to letting all those expensively-won sales leads simply dribble away.

Press conferences

There are pros and cons for press conferences at exhibitions. Against holding one are the facts that journalists are very busy and the danger of your story getting lost in the sheer weight of information being bandied about during a show. In favour is the fact that the journalists you want to attend are probably already at the show and the fact that what you have to say will be of relevance to the special interests of show participants.

Your story needs to be a fairly strong one. If it is, a press conference can be a good idea and can be run with less problems at a show than usual.

Press conferences at exhibitions should be:

- kept short, under half an hour if possible
- flagged up to the press well in advance of the exhibition
- highlighted with a strong notice on the press office notice board
- double-managed at the exhibition – you need someone to co-ordinate the conference and someone in the press office to shepherd journalists in the right direction.

Pressing the flesh

You may have arranged to get journalists onto your stand and you may be able to contact journalists through the press office.

You may feel that this is enough but really an active PR operator at an exhibition should be prowling the show and making sure that he picks up on as many journalists as is humanly possible. This is one time when virtually all your key trade journals and special interest publications will be available for face-to-face meetings at one time. It's a great opportunity to line up future feature articles, arrange plant visits and generally build relationships with the media. Use it.

Daily debriefs

Exhibitions are tiring. The wear and tear of being on one's feet for hours at a stretch is in itself enough to ensure that stand staff are shattered at the end of the day, never mind the adrenaline surge of dealing with customers one after another. Even so it is very important to have a daily debrief on how things are going and what's gone wrong.

We haven't gone into the logistics of setting up exhibition participating simply because it is beyond the scope of a discussion of public relations and because the wealth of detail is formidable. Because there are so many things that can go wrong some will, some major and some trivial. Nothing is ever perfect on the first day. It's worth having a daily review because you can be improving performance throughout the show and daily exhaustion should not mean spoiling the ship for a halfpenny's worth of tar.

It may seem a little arbitrary to include speaker opportunities in the same chapter as exhibitions, after all, the requirements for setting up a speaker programme appear to be rather different from those of exploiting an exhibition presence. There are, of course, massive differences but there are also similarities. It is no accident that exhibitions frequently contain an add-on conference element, or that a number of conferences have small exhibitions attached to them. An exhibition stand is a public exposure of a company and a poor stand can do severe damage, just as a good one can win credit – so too with conference participation where you're better off staying home than giving a poor presentation. The attendance at each have a lot in common in that they have a definite interest in the subject of the exhibition or conference and have made a degree of commitment to attend. They are, in fact, a key and committed audience.

Just as with exhibitions, there are opportunities to build additional PR advantage. A well-produced speech or presentation can provide the basis for general issue of a press release and may be suitable for reproduction as a feature article. It may also be possible to gain press interest and coverage from prompted attendance at the speech.

Unlike exhibitions, however, ensuring participation in a conference is not simply a matter of making a booking. Speaking opportunities usually have to be actively sought.

89

There are a number of ways of identifying speaking opportunities which may prove of value, three of which are comparatively straightforward:

- professional conference organisers are continually on the look-out for good speakers and will readily supply lists of forward conferences. They can be approached over particular conferences and should also be supplied with background details on possible speakers, together with areas of expertise, for consideration at the planning stage of possible conferences

- all of the trade exhibitions which cover an organisation's areas of operation are worth considering. Though not all will have conferences associated with them, a number will. Speakers do not necessarily have to be exhibitors

- professional groups, trade associations, commercial and business interest groups, for example Chambers of Trade and Commerce etc all provide speaking opportunities. It is worth considering which may be relevant to one's organisation and investigating the possibilities. Some will simply not be worth the time and trouble but some may provide a relevant and strong platform.

There is a limit to how much 'speechifying' one can expect senior executives to do and there is a limit to how effectively one can use a large number of speaking opportunities, particularly if one is looking to the extra mileage provided by press release and feature material. A speaking opportunity programme, just like an exhibition programme, needs to be selective and allow one to take advantage of any given opportunity to the full.

Selection is a matter of judging the quality of the likely audience, the general importance of the event and the possibilities which are offered for spin-off coverage. Timing, too, may be relevant if a conference allows one to make an important announcement – a fact of which politicians are particularly aware.

This is not the place to discuss the skills of presentation; they already fill several books in their own right. In essence the main points are very simple:

- prepare carefully
- check contents with a neutral observer
- structure your speech (tell them what you're going to say, say it and then tell them what you've said)
- use visuals if possible
- rehearse until you're totally confident of your subject
- project strongly when presenting; a speech is a performance.

For the PR man, who may well have to write the speech in the first place, the rules for maximising benefit are also pretty simple:

- don't even think of using a speaker who is not a proven performer
- if you're responsible for producing the text of the speech, remember the spoken word is very different to the written word and write accordingly (a good speech writer will work to the speech patterns of the speaker and will employ a sense of timing very like a dramatist, or stand-up comedian)
- give everyone plenty of warning and time to prepare,

speaker, slide provider, conference organiser, any press invitees etc

- try to build in a clear news angle on which to hang follow-up releases
- Make sure texts of the speech are available on the day for press and delegate use
- try, and this can be hard, to ensure the speaker understands that this is a commercial communications opportunity and not an ego trip.

Speakers invest a lot of time, effort and, importantly, something of themselves in making presentations. They should not be expected to make this commitment lightly and every speaking opportunity should be carefully judged for merit and then exploited to the full. Like so many aspects of PR dividends result from care in thinking a programme through and further care in making it work. More than most things, a speaking programme is not worth doing, indeed is damaging all round, if it's not worked on. It can be effective, particularly when you are dealing with narrow or well-defined target audiences, when done well.

91

15

Sponsorship and corporate hospitality

If you become involved in sponsorship then you almost certainly also get involved in corporate hospitality. The reverse is not true. A corporate hospitality programme doesn't necessarily involve sponsorship at all. Nonetheless sponsorship and corporate hospitality tend to go hand-in-hand. They are usually financed out of the same budget within an organisation. They are both treated as something which falls into an intermediate area somewhere between below the line promotion, sales, marketing and public relations and they both usually finish up being a PR responsibility.

The public relations function is, at the end of the day, probably the right place for responsibility to be placed, if only because a PR operative is likely to be the best person qualified to handle the logistics of such operations.

There may be a number of reasons why an organisation decides to sponsor an event, and some of them may not relate too directly to the benefits obtained – it's surprising how often a corporate sponsorship relates to the Chairman's personal leisure interests. In general, though, sponsorship is undertaken for one of two reasons:

- it provides a vehicle for clear branding by an organisation and a consequent high level of exposure

- it provides an opportunity to hang other valuable activities onto the sponsorship which are of benefit to the organisation (usually corporate hospitality but not necessarily).

(There may be other valid reasons which apply to smaller sponsorships such as supporting a major customer's event or playing one's part in the local community, but such special circumstances are not really to be seen as part of a sponsorship programme in the normal sense, any more than taking a congratulatory advertisement in a local newspaper supplement to support a feature about a customer can be regarded as part of mainstream advertising.)

Whichever of the two main reasons for entering into a sponsorship, the very first thing to recognise is that paying for the sponsorship is merely the beginning. If you're not prepared to support your initial investment and deliberately set out to make the sponsorship work for you then you would probably have done better to keep your money in your pocket in the first place.

93

There is a brief discussion of the Mars sponsorship of the London Marathon in Chapter 25, and this may be regarded as a classic illustration of the successful supporting of a sponsorship investment, particularly when it is contrasted with the relative lack of benefit which previous sponsors obtained. The world of sponsorship is littered with examples of large investments which provided small returns and small investments which provided large returns and most of the time the reason for this happening is a reflection of the degree of commitment of the sponsor.

What you have bought with a sponsorship is primarily an opportunity. For major sponsorships a very rough guideline is that whatever it cost to buy the sponsorship, be prepared to spend the same amount again to make it work for you. This additional spend will be in a number of ways, and may, indeed, exceed the cost of the sponsorship, particularly if you have a large corporate hospitality operation planned.

(For some sponsorships the related additional expenditure may be massively larger than the cost of buying in the first place, but this tends to be atypical and what you believe yourself to have invested may well depend on internal accounting procedures –

for example if you tie a massive sales promotion, or special offer programme, to a sponsorship, it is not really an additional spend but simply a switch within a promotional budget from one type of promotion to another.)

Sponsorship is normally associated with some form of entertainment or leisure activity, very frequently sport, in people's minds and, of course, this is very often the case. However, there are a great number of areas other than entertainment which are worth considering. Academic sponsorships, for example, may make a great deal of sense to companies with an important research base – aiding links with the university-based research communities, encouraging recruitment and identifying the company with academic excellence in the minds of its publics. Sponsorship of charities or charity events clearly has a number of positive associations for an organisation, though one would hope that PR benefits are not a prime reason for such support. The sponsorship of appropriate awards and prizes may also produce positive and relevant associations; indeed the Booker award for novels is one of the most successful sponsorships around, though the links between the world of books and the food importing and plantation managing sponsors remain somewhat obscure. Sponsorship of specific industry awards, presentation dinners and the like can work well too, particularly where the aim is to raise one's profile with a relatively small, tightly defined group.

However it is entertainment and particularly sport which has seen sponsorship activity grow to a massive industry with budgets of quite massive proportions being spent on occasion. This growth in the sponsorship business has been fuelled by a number of factors which include the way in which sport is now marketed aggressively to an ever-increasing watching public, and a parallel relaxation of the rules governing the 'branding' of events by sponsors.

To justify the sort of expenditure involved on sponsorships, large and small, sponsors have become increasingly aware of the need to look for additional benefit, beyond simple branding,

94

from their investment. Of course, popular entertainment offers this with the opportunities to combine a programme of corporate hospitality with one's sponsorship – whether it be a box at a racetrack to watch a sponsored race or an entire entertainment suite for the duration of the Olympic Games (sponsors of the 1992 Barcelona Olympics took over entire hotels for the duration or brought in cruise liners to act as their own private floating hotels in the harbour).

A prime reason for wishing to sponsor an event, whether it be large or small, is because of the positive associations which such a sponsorship will provide and the exposure which will be gained through such an association. In order to make sure that the sponsorship delivers what one expects of it there are a number of considerations which should be taken into account from the very start.

A fundamental consideration must be the appropriateness of the sponsorship. Your organisation will have a corporate positioning and, hopefully, a clear idea of the way in which it wishes to be seen. If a possible sponsorship does not fit with this then, no matter how good a deal it may appear, you should not accept it. Publicity and exposure is not, by definition, good – no matter what some showbiz press agents think – and the wrong sort of association can do as much harm as good.

95

A second key consideration must be how far a sponsorship can be used as a hook on which to hang additional activities. Are there corporate entertainment opportunities? Can you link the sponsorship into other promotional activities through special offers, premium giveaways etc? Can you use the fact of sponsorship to 'brand' and add perceived value to your products? (Such chances can be as varied as 'sponsors of the xyz software award' carried by a pc producer to 'Official Snack Food of the Olympic Games' on a packet of confectionery.) Can the sponsorship be used to add impact to your mainstream advertising? Can the sponsorship be used to enhance a dealer support programme? . . . The list of possible add-ons can be very considerable but, in the final analysis, may be what makes a sponsorship viable or not.

A third consideration is certain to be one of checking just what is being offered in the sponsorship package. If you are primarily after media exposure then you need to know, and to bargain hard from the very start. What coverage is already lined up in terms of TV deals? What are the rules on physical branding, for example board placement or participant's clothing, and have these been cleared with the relevant TV coverage? Critically important, is your name included as an integral part of the title? (The difference between 'The World Tiddlywinks Championships sponsored by Muggins' and 'The Muggins World Tiddlywinks Title' is critical in all coverage, press and broadcast.) What limitation are placed on the sponsor's use of the title of the event and on claims which can be made about the event?

Once you have made the deal and signed up the sponsorship don't rely on the promoter to publicise it for you. He probably won't do as good a job as you can on publicising the event itself, partly because his interest in exposure is more limited than yours in that any coverage for the event is satisfactory whether or not it is branded by the sponsor. He certainly won't do a particularly good job on publicising your involvement, after all he's largely fulfilled his obligation by making the deal with you.

All this applies on the grand scale of major events but it also applies at a more minor level and, if anything, the smaller sponsorships require a greater pro-rata effort from the sponsor to exploit the publicity opportunity. If you want people to know that you're sponsoring the 3.30 race at York, for example, you need to work at it in every area other than the simple listings on the racing pages.

Seek to create PR opportunities around the event, trailer stories, background features, photo opportunities. Flag up your sponsorship through all your own available channels of communication and by 'branding' all forms of routine communication. Involve your staff, both as an employee relations exercise and to make them messengers on behalf of the sponsorship. In the same way involve your dealers, retail outlets, agents and all your commercial contacts. Work very closely with the promoter's publicity machine to create interest and to ensure that you brand everything they do – and be prepared for continual negotiation on this point. Let the promoter know, in no uncertain terms, all the extra work you are putting in to ensure the success of his event and look for quid pro quo benefits in return. In fact work your involvement to the extreme if you expect to get a proper turn on investment.

A few paragraphs ago we suggested, rather slightingly, that one reason behind sponsorships can be the personal interest of the Chairman or Chief Executive in an event or a type of activity. Well, now we've indicated the kind of support that is needed to make a sponsorship work, it's time to admit that such interest can be a pretty good extra reason for picking a sponsorship. It may be the one guarantee that you can get that the level of resources which you need to make a sponsorship work will, in fact, be available to you!

Corporate entertainment goes hand in hand with sponsorship, but you don't need to sponsor an event to make use of it for corporate entertainment, as the hospitality tents which crowd around every major sporting event in this country, or the block bookings for seats at Covent Garden testify.

There are a number of overlaps in considerations which should be taken into account however. Is the entertainment appropriate to your organisation and to your selected guests? How can you make the fact of offering corporate entertainment work for you beyond the obvious offering of some hospitality? What additional things can you do to make your investment provide an extra reward?

One important consideration you may wish to take into account when organising corporate entertainment is how much opportunity there will be to interface with your guests. It can be very money wasting to lay on entertainment at some expense and then find there is no chance to even meet the people on whom you have spent the money – a problem faced at events such as golf tournaments where your guests may spend virtually all their time well away from you, following their favourite around the course. So plan the programme to ensure at least some contact.

Another aspect of this question of guest contact is making sure that such contact works for you by remembering an important rule: *you and your staff are not there to have fun, you're there to work and any fun is a bonus.* The sight of an organisation's representatives talking to each other and generally having a good time while ignoring guests at an event which has cost good money and much effort is all too often to be seen.

Corporate entertainment is a way of meeting precisely those people you want to, in an environment which you have chosen, and with you in the position of the host. In a way it relates to sponsorship rather as direct mail relates to general advertising and, in the same way, it is much more expensive in terms of each individual contacted. It is very important that you make this highly favourable situation and this expensive one-to-one contact work properly for you and you will only achieve this with careful planning and a good deal of follow through. Here is the great common factor with sponsorship in general: *It is not the initial investment which brings results but the extent to whichyou are prepared to go to make that initial investment work for you.*

One last thought about money. Both sponsorship and corporate entertainment present clear chances to win goodwill and increase mutual understanding. They are PR exercises, but the spin off benefits which they offer for direct advertising and promotion and for sales contact are such that any PR person worth their salt will make sure that they are financed, at least in part, out of the advertising and sales budgets.

16

Print and publications

There is one overwhelmingly appealing aspect to the whole area of printed material which you produce yourself as part of a PR programme. You are totally in charge.

When you produce something for yourself no journalist is going to get between you and your ultimate audience and rewrite your words. No TV editor is going to cut out the part of the film where your logo is proudly displayed for all to see. No unexpected news event is going to break, leaving your press conference empty and your story buried on the inside pages. No sudden cloudburst is going to reduce your corporate hospitality outing to Henley to a rain sodden afternoon in a chilly tent watching Wimbledon on the TV. It's nice, as the British Gas advertisements say, to be in control.

There is a wide range of printed materials which are used directly or indirectly in managing one's public relations. After all, as we have argued, everything produced by an organisation impinges on PR in one way or another. So perhaps it's not silly or an example of self-aggrandizement to argue that a public relations officer should be involved in documents as far removed from his direct responsibility as instruction leaflets. Perhaps it's also reasonable that a list of 'PR Literature' in a widely respected text book should include postage stamps!

For our purposes, however, it will be more productive to narrow the focus a bit. Rather than attempting to produce an exhaustive list of 'PR Literature', from desk diaries to the headings on press release paper, let's just accept the general point that all printed material has a PR overtone, and look more closely at some of the more important uses of print as part of the PR armoury.

Let's also agree that, in this context, we're not looking to become expert print buyers – so there's no discussion of the difference between letterpress and web-offset or gravure, no explanation of pantone colours, not even a list of accepted proofreader's correction marks. If you're going to buy a lot of print, then these may be things you need to learn but mostly, with the exception of proofing marks, you won't need this kind of knowledge because it's readily available from your designer and from your print suppliers themselves.

There are a number of areas of printwork which are central to PR activity and which recur time and again in the planning of a PR programme.

100

Newsletters

Newsletters come in two main forms, external and internal. It is nearly always a mistake to try to merge the two into a single publication because the perspectives of the target publics are simply not sufficiently similar, as we look at briefly in Chapter 19.

A newsletter demands the same skills for production as does a newspaper and follows much the same rules for presentation in terms of layout, editorial style and content balance. Of course, there is one essential difference. A newsletter has a single, unvarying point of view and reason for existence – that of the organisation producing it.

The essential trick with a newsletter is to succeed in producing a publication which has all the newsiness and ease of reading which one expects from a commercial publication while drawing on a severely limited information base and maintaining a single editorial standpoint.

Newsletters offer a number of benefits which are simply not

found in other forms of communication. By separating themselves from the clearly promotional approach of brochures or direct mail shots, newsletters create an impression of reasoned, objective comment – people tend to read newsletters with their guard down. Because of their format and style newsletters can go into subjects in depth in a way that is not available to one in other forms of communication. A well-written newsletter can cover a whole range of subjects and communicate a range of messages all in a single readable document.

Obviously the time, trouble and cost of producing a newsletter is only justified if one has a reasonably large circulation, so this is not an option for dealing with small specialist groups. In fact there is a general rule with printed material that the unit cost drops dramatically with the length of the print run, particularly where relatively small numbers, a few thousand, are involved, so overall costs of producing 5,000 copies of a publication are not likely to be significantly different from producing 1,000, perhaps 15 per cent up (this does not apply to the same extent where specialist print processes such as silk screen are used or where there is a manual element in production such as folding and gluing enclosure flaps).

101

Newsletters can vary in complexity of production from fully fledged newspapers through to quite simple four-page, A4-size documents. The production complications can be similarly variable from full newspaper production down to desk top publishing which offers a cheap and effective means of setting up a newsletter from scratch.

Content is always going to be more important than presentation with a newsletter and, once you have established the style for the first issue, design and layout for subsequent issues is a relatively straightforward matter. It's therefore worth investing money in getting the first issue professionally designed and also getting a series of style rules to be applied for the future as part of the initial design package.

The approach to content should be that of the journalist and should aim to produce a mix of news and feature material much as one gets in a newspaper, with the changes of pace, length and style which provide a varied read. What you write about will be determined by who your readers are and will determine the overall approach and style. Good newsletters, however, have in common that same balance and variation in pace, which can be found in successful newspapers from the *Times* to the *Mirror*.

Annual report and accounts

This is the one big annual opportunity for publicly listed companies to make a major splash, spell out the background to their financial performance, and share plans and aspirations with shareholders and all other interested parties. From being purely financial explanations, annual reports and accounts have developed into lavishly produced documents, carefully designed and written, and ideally projecting the strongest corporate identity possible for an organisation.

The requirement for such documents was originally a legal one for listed companies, but such has been the perceived PR power of this type of publication that many other organisations which are not public limited companies have adopted the practice of issuing annual report and accounts as a PR and communications exercise.

If you're dealing with a genuine annual report and accounts it makes sense to use one of the number of specialist printers operating in this area, not merely for quality of work but for a full understanding of the handling of figures which will remain confidential right up to publication and a proper understanding of the formal content of the document throughout.

Corporate literature

A support to sales literature and all other printed material from an organisation, the corporate brochure or range of corporate literature allows a full organisational positioning and 'in depth' information on an organisation. It is a classic piece of PR material in that it does not seek to sell anything direct but simply to position and explain an organisation. As the central statement of what an organisation is, this is a document which should not be attempted on the cheap.

These days corporate brochures tend to go hand-in-hand with corporate videos which can be used repeatedly for presentations, meetings, background information and even cannibalised for bits of TV footage.

The same two warnings should be made about corporate brochures and corporate videos:

- having made what is likely to be a substantial investment in producing them, don't let them sit on the shelf but actively seek opportunities to use them
- don't forget they need updating so try to design them for a reasonably long life span in the first place and be prepared to bite the bullet of updating and reproducing once in a while – an outdated corporate presentation has exactly the opposite effect to the one intended.

103

Article and press coverage reprints

You put a lot of work into placing articles and news stories, so make them work for you as often as possible. Reprinted articles and collections of strong press cuttings can make powerful direct mail shots for external use and valuable motivational/informative publications for use within an organisation and with close outside contacts such as dealers and distributors.

Media support material

If you're running any sort of media relations campaign then there will be a range of pieces of printwork which you will probably need to use and which will be a direct tool of the PR department working in its most typical mode. This range will include press release paper, information folders or wallets for press kits, and possibly standardised background material for briefings.

A sound rule to follow in all this is to keep it simple. The media doesn't want to have to pick its way through elaborate letterheads to find the start of a story and is generally pretty unimpressed by design concepts. By the same token don't make press releases or backgrounders look too 'printy' even if your wonderful desk top system allows you to do this as rapidly as producing them in a simply typewriter style face – overproduced press material doesn't look right and doesn't feel right and, above all, has no sense of newsiness so journalists don't like it and tend to assume it's advertising matter of no urgency.

104

As for the rest of the printed material which an organisation produces, it should certainly conform to corporate identity guidelines and agreed messages and should never conflict with the agreed PR approaches of a company. You'll probably be responsible for the production of some of it, for inputs into some of it and, if you have a corporate identity policy, for policing all of it. It can be a fascinating field and it's very easy to get deeply involved in the world of print through from graphic design to the mechanical processes of the printing presses. The only problem with becoming too intimately involved is that it leaves you very little time to get on with the rest of the PR programme. This is a field where a little technical knowledge may prove to be less of a dangerous thing than too much.

17

Advertising as a PR weapon

We looked, some way back in this general discussion of PR, at definitions of what PR is all about and by and large accepted the IPR wording of 'establishing and maintaining mutual understanding and goodwill between an organisation and its publics'. Hardly the way to describe the role of advertising in the normal promotional programme of an organisation, it would seem, and yet there are times when advertising becomes a PR weapon rather than a direct promotional activity.

The skills which the advertising industry bring to bear can be very considerable and very specific. The degree of expertise to be found in most serious advertising agencies is considerable, as is the creative flair. Budgets spent on advertising tend to be much greater than those spent on managing public relations. It's hardly surprising, then, that advertising people fiercely resist any suggestion that their discipline should be subsumed into PR. Nor is it surprising that PR people sometimes cast envious eyes at their colleagues in advertising and try to get hold of some portion of their legendary budgets.

The debate is sometimes conducted as to whether PR delivers better value for money than advertising and, therefore, whether budgets should be switched, and such discussion may occasionally be legitimate. But mostly all this in-fighting is nonsense. Advertising performs one role, PR another. The skills and background knowledge of PR people and advertising people have something in common but they are different. PR firms rarely run good advertising campaigns and advertising agencies are rarely any good at PR. (Always be very wary indeed of the advertising agency which offers to throw in PR for free or at a very low cost as a bolt-on to the advertising service which they provide.)

There are circumstances, however, where 'above the line' advertising can have a valuable role to play in a PR campaign. ('Above the line' is an advertising term which originates from the layout of invoices from agencies. It refers to advertising carried in bought space as opposed to 'below the line' which refers to point of sale, direct mail etc.) The use of bought advertising in a PR campaign is a way of disseminating a message widely in precisely the form in which one wishes the message to be carried. Unlike media relations work, there is no intermediate interpreter or sub-editor. Unlike one-to-one communication, direct mail, newsletters etc a wide audience can be reached at relatively low unit cost.

106

There are two main sets of circumstances in which one may well wish to use advertising techniques for what are, essentially, PR ends. These are when you are looking to make a rapid impact on the attitudes of a large or relatively inaccessible public or when you have a formal need to impart factual information and cannot risk this information being distorted or not published.

Mounting a campaign to influence opinion across a wide sector of the public and knowing that your message is going to reach the greater part of that public on more than one occasion is very hard to achieve with any degree of certainty unless you are prepared to pay for media space. Doing so should not be seen as being instead of utilising the other mainstream techniques of PR which we have looked at earlier but as a means of reinforcing them and with a guarantee of the chance to publicise your message, if not of having that message accepted.

Where you need to guarantee receipt of some information by the public or some sector of the public then you may have to take complete control of the process of dissemination yourself. It's most unusual for the process of calling a press conference or issuing a press release to provide a certainty that your news will be carried. Advertising provides that certainty.

Examples of the opinion influencing form of advertising are:

- the range of corporate advertising undertaken by companies to emphasise aspects of their operation which reflect creditably on them, but which do not stimulate any particular purchase decision, for example corporate 'greenness', international strength, technical expertise etc
- advertising carried in support of, or in opposition to, contested takeover bids
- issue advertising by pressure groups, or their targets, for example Friends of the Earth, British Nuclear Fuels.

Examples of the purely information dissemination advertisements (though these influence opinion too) are:

- crisis communication advertising following a product recall or product safety scare
- 'tombstone' announcements of interim and final results for quoted companies.

Now this type of advertising is fundamentally different from the promotion of products or services. The decision to invest in producing such campaigns is determined by the communication needs of a company, rather than the sales needs and, most of the time, by a wish to influence attitudes and opinions – 'establish mutual understanding and goodwill', if you like. The justification for the expenditure involved is not a matter of looking at sales graphs or market share, and the thinking behind producing such advertising is likely to be precisely the same thinking which influences the structure of a PR programme.

The decision to use advertising as a PR weapon is not one to be undertaken lightly. Advertising can be very expensive. Advertising is very effective when it comes to selling product but lacks the credibility of editorial. It might even be argued that advertising some views actually weakens one's case because the public has developed a cynicism about anything said in an advertisement. All this may be true but advertising delivers control and it delivers guarantees of exposure and there are times when this is precisely what a PR operation needs.

When this is the case it becomes sensible to think of the advertising operation as part of the PR campaign and to allow a proper and serious PR input into the content, approach and placement of the ads. This is not to say that the ads should be produced by the PR department or by the PR consultancy. Unless a PR function has a proven track record in advertising, as is sometimes the case for specialist investor relations companies who handle takeovers, flotations and publication or results, then it is plain madness to use PR people to produce advertisements when one has advertising people available. What one needs to do is to put the PR people into the role of client, even if they are in a consultancy, and make them part of the team briefing the advertising agency.

108

Failure to do this will cause problems and, almost certainly, result in mixed messages. Just as it is necessary for public relations considerations to be integrated into a total marketing communications programme when one is practising marketing PR, so it is necessary for advertising to be completely integrated into a public or corporate relations programme when one is concerned with issues of mutual understanding and goodwill.

All this may seem to be rather obvious and so it is when looked at in the calm of theoretical discussion. In practice the arguments which develop between advertising and PR over the issues of corporate advertising, issue advertising and service advertising have, on occasion, to be seen to be believed. Much of the time these arguments spring from a simple confusion between ends and means. If the ends are properly regarded as PR ends then advertising should become a servant of the PR function but, just because it meets a PR need, there's no reason for its implementation to be carried through by PR people.

Demarkation disputes, with their overtones of trade union arguments of the 1960s and 70s, may be understandable but they are not productive and they have no place in the practice of PR or, indeed, of advertising. Making sure that the people who carry through a task are competent to do so does.

This whole business of division between advertising and PR revisits the earlier discussion of the marketing mix and an insistence that PR should be seen as an integrated part of the marketing communications programme. If we come at this from another angle we can see, equally clearly, that advertising forms a part of an organisation's overall communications mix. There are specific circumstances in which advertising may be used as a PR tool. There are no circumstances in which advertising, the approach adopted, the messages projected and the targets at which it is aimed do not have an impact on public perceptions of a company.

The arguments for a company to integrate its total communications strategy, provide consistent messages and consider the cross-effects between different strands of communications activity are, I think, compelling. This is no argument for advertising activity to be subsumed into the PR function. That would be absurd. It is, however, an argument that it is a major mistake for organisations to regard PR as a totally separate and unrelated discipline or to regard PR as some sort of poor relation.

109

18

Corporate identity

Intro?

Everything which an organisation does or says – every bit of printed material which it issues, every sign which it paints on the side of its transport, the look of its stationery, the form of its sales literature, its annual report and accounts – says something about that organisation and leaves an impression with anyone coming in contact with it.

110

If all these things have some degree of coherence and produce a consistent impression then an organisation might be said to have a corporate identity, or at least a corporate image. If they don't, then one is entitled to ask the question 'why not?'. It's a question to which there may be any number of perfectly good answers and it is by no means certain that the creation of a corporate image for an organisation is a 'good thing' in any absolute sense. However, in the absence of any such good reason the organisation which fails to project itself through the presentation of a consistent 'face' to the world is almost certainly missing out on an opportunity to win friends and influence people.

Actually the same argument was set out earlier, which said that an organisation has 'public relations' like it or not, and the only question, whether or not to manage them, applies equally to corporate identity. Of course an organisation has an identity independent of anything it does to formalise or project this and, rather less strongly, it also has an 'image' even if this image consists of a whole series of disparate bits and pieces.

There can be a great deal of semantic argument about the use of terms like 'corporate identity' and 'corporate image' and the terms are used in slightly different ways by different people, notably graphic designers, advertising people, management consultants and PR men. Let's, therefore, be clear about how they are being used here.

'Corporate image' is being used to cover the style adopted by an organisation in its visual presentation – covering anything relating to the company which might be described as being 'designed'.

'Corporate identity' is being used to describe the formal presentation of a company, incorporating corporate image but also including any formal positioning, objectives, mission statements or principles which exist, together with any other overt manifestations of corporate style (covering everything from the famous IBM dress code to the 'no reserved car spaces, no executive dining rooms, no separate offices' egalitarianism of the Mars Corporation). Such a definition of corporate identity is a limiting one but recognises that identity is not limited to a question of graphics, while at the same time not making it such a catch-all term that everything about an organisation is subsumed into it – we have earlier used 'corporate reputation' for this general description which is a more accurate reflection of what some PR people mean when they talk about corporate identity.

111

Corporate identity, in these terms, is something which can be tightly controlled and which can be made to work for an organisation by providing it with recognisable symbols and a recognisable style by which it is identified. That such symbols and style should reflect on the organisation positively goes without saying. That such symbols and style will be meaningless, even harmful, if they do not reflect the reality of an organisation should be similarly obvious.

Assuming that there is no overriding wish to avoid too consistent a presentation of an organisation to the outside world, deliberate separation of individual brands for example, then the benefits from ensuring the presentation of a consistent 'face' to the world can be considerable.

At its simplest level there is benefit to be gained from straight-forward repetition. The more your face is seen and recognised then the more awareness there is that you are a serious operator and a force to be reckoned with. Along with this recognition there goes a general feeling of security and con-fidence. The vast majority of people prefer to deal with the known rather than the unknown, not simply in terms of buying products but in every way, from seeking employment through to picking shares for their PEP.

More subtly, the type of face which is presented to the world creates an impression of who you are and what you stand for. When this impression is divorced from reality then it does you little good since you are either projecting an impression which is irrelevant and, therefore, unhelpful or you are, effectively, telling a lie, and liars, with some notable exceptions, tend to get found out. When this impression is a reflection of reality it can reinforce and help establish perceptions which are directly helpful to your business.

112

If this sounds a bit esoteric then simply think about the way corporate images abound in the everyday world and how they impact on our perceptions of the organisations involved. An organisation such as Virgin, with its youthful and dynamic positioning and product range aimed primarily at leisure interests, would look somewhat silly with a graphic present-ation which reflected long-established, somewhat conservative values and similarly any of our major financial institutions would find a corporate logo of the style adopted by Virgin somewhat inappropriate. In fact what has happened to the corporate logos of Britain's main clearing banks, and how these logos have been used over the years, has reflected the move-ment of the banks into a more competitive retail environment in a fascinating way. The black horse which encourages us to see Lloyds Bank as a provider of birth-to-death financial services, including mortgages, insurance, savings schemes and a range of account options, is a very different animal from the black horse which stood guard over the slightly intimidating high street bank of 30 years ago. Equally fascinating has been the development of the Shell logo over the years where the changes made have successfully presented us with an immediately recognisable logo which has never been allowed to become 'dated' in appearance – a continuum of change which has so well preserved the essential visual 'sign' of the company that many would swear it has not been altered at all, despite very considerable and fairly frequent modifications.

The corporate image of an organisation normally starts with the corporate logotype, known as the logo, which may be thought of as the symbol of the organisation and which provides a focal starting point for all design considerations. The conventional wisdom is that historically such logos derive from the clan symbols behind which the warriors of an army went into battle, or which were emblazoned on the shields and armour of the leaders. Certainly they developed through the livery of various shipping and transport companies in a tradition which continues today and which is seen at its most flamboyant with a variety of airlines. There are other less romantic strands which may also lead to the corporate logo, however, notably the practice of craftsmen and, later, factories to brand products with a mark of origin, and the practice of elaborating simple identification signs on factories into more elaborate pieces of sign writing which could also act as advertisements.

113

Today almost every organisation of any size has developed some form of corporate logo, and this has become an extremely lucrative business for a number of specialist design firms – at the top end of the market 'corporate identities', as designers are wont to describe them, can be quite mind-blowingly expensive.

What is less general is following through with the use of the logo once one has got it. It's not enough to get some pretty piece of design and attempt to graft it onto one's existing printed material, livery, signs etc. If one is going to take a corporate image seriously then it needs to be applied right across an organisation's operations, and this really means that one needs to develop some form of central applications manual. Such a manual will cover precise colour instructions, with pantone

Footnote!

references, for the use of the logo; rules on use of the logo for various applications, brochures, stationery, vehicle livery, signs, fascias etc; alternatives for single colour usage; prohibitions on use of the logo etc. It should also extend beyond the use of the logo itself to cover general presentation rules for the corporate image – setting out house style for such matters as layout of correspondence, preferred range of typefaces to be used in literature, possibly covering any standard 'strap lines' or promotional slogans used by the organisation etc.

Once you have a clearly defined design for corporate presentation and a comprehensive set of rules for its application then you have the means to implement a corporate image. Once you have established a corporate image, then you've gone a long way towards establishing a corporate identity.

A purely design approach is not, in itself, going to provide you with a corporate image, even in the restricted sense in which we are using the term here. There needs, if you like, to be content as well as style for image to become identity. Put somewhat simplisticly, a beautiful livery won't say much on a filthy dirty van and an elegantly laid-out brochure will have little impact if the words are gobbledygook.

In terms of corporate identity this means that there need to be some clear statements of what an organisation does, what it stands for and what it aspires to in addition to what it looks like. These are usually given titles such as 'corporate positioning', 'mission statement' or 'corporate philosophy' and they are an integral part of corporate identity. Such positioning for an organisation is not something to be written down and filed away in a corporate planning file, or hung on the wall of the chairman's office. It needs to be carried through into all of the various forms of communication conducted by the organisation, set out for the employees, explained and amplified to all of an organisation's publics and absorbed into the very fabric of the organisational culture.] ᴗQuote on brand book

Corporate identity in this sense informs and influences all of an organisation's public relations and how they are managed.

Without a visual coherence for an organisation, a corporate image, it becomes far more difficult to develop this idea of a corporate identity but the corporate image is an expression of, not a substitute for, a far more fundamental notion.

Now most organisations, unless they are in a state of considerable internal turmoil or inefficiency, do have a definite idea of their own identity – who they are, what they set out to achieve, what principles they operate by. The formal creation of a corporate identity is no more than an expression of this in a way which allows others to understand and appreciate. (The act of creating such an identity may help clarify existing thinking, but this is a spin off benefit.) Like all aspects of PR practice, a corporate identity cannot alter the reality on which it is based. What it can do is to reveal and project that reality in the most favourable light. In common with all management of public relations it is an exercise in influencing perceptions to ensure that you get the best reputation to which you are entitled.

115

19

Special publics, community and employee relations

We have seen, and taken as given, that any organisation has a range of publics with which it will wish to communicate and build understanding. Some of the specialist disciplines which have developed within PR, notably public affairs and investor or City relations, are no more than a reflection of the existence of such special publics.

We also have to recognise that the interests of each definable public with which an organisation deals will be different. Consequently the PR messages which one wishes to project to them, the techniques used, the tone of voice adopted and, even, the final objectives of the PR programme will also be different.

For many special publics the differences will be sufficiently subtle for it to make sense to ignore them – one can get altogether too sophisticated in segmenting the target audiences for PR work. For many PR activities the spread is such that a number of separate special publics are covered by the same activity. There are, however, at least two such special publics whose interests are liable to be radically different from the others. They are both close to home and, although they may be aware of, and influenced by, PR activities aimed at the big world out there, 'out there' is precisely where they are not.

The local community within which an organisation is situated and the people who are actually part of the organisation make up two very important publics who are very close to home indeed. Community relations and employee relations are not the same thing but they often overlap greatly and, for an organisation which is a major employer in an area, it is quite impossible to see where the one starts and the other finishes.

In both cases, certainly with employee relations and probably with community relations, there will be a starting point of identification with the organisation and, hopefully, a degree of shared pleasure in achievement and hope for the future. The organisation which cannot command a degree of loyalty from the people who look to it for their livelihoods probably has an employee relations problem which goes far beyond anything which can be seriously affected by internal PR activity. It is less certain that the local community will take pride in the achievements of a local company but is far more likely to be the case than not.

117

For both these groups, then, it is reasonable to assume a degree of interest in any information supplied and a degree of sympathy for an organisation's point of view. It is not, however, reasonable to assume that there is total concurrence between the views of employees and the views of an organisation as a corporate entity, nor is it reasonable to take employee goodwill for granted. The same applies, but even more strongly to the local community where understanding and goodwill may have to be worked for very hard, particularly where an organisation has business practices or aims which are not totally at one with local residents' wishes – pollution, traffic, building programmes etc.

The two groups have similarities in their likely viewpoints. There will be physical overlap in the individual and family membership of each group. There is a further link via a third sub-group which may be thought of as being half-and-half – local suppliers of services and products who, while not strictly employees, have a direct economic link to an organisation. This overlap can be important and may affect the content of employee relations and community relations programmes. Nonetheless the groups are separate and it makes sense to look at the sort of activities which one might undertake to communicate with each separately also.

Employee relations activities

No single thing damages the relationship between an organisation and its employees (management and employees if one prefers but, since 'management' is such a variable term it is easier to think of an organisation as a corporate entity and anyone who works for it as an employee) as a feeling of not knowing what is going on. At best a feeling that one is being kept in ignorance makes it hard to fully identify with an organisation; at worst one imagines all sorts of unlikely things; rumour is king and distrust and suspicion rule.

118   Employee communications, then, is a matter of keeping people informed as far as is practicable about the organisation, what it is doing, and why it is doing it. It is also a matter of seeking to strengthen the bonds which people feel with the organisation by reinforcing their feeling of belonging.

There is an anomaly which is integral to the whole notion of the relationship between an organisation and its employees. On the one hand the organisation is a separate corporate entity in its own right while, on the other hand, the employees actually *are* the organisation, or at least a significant part of it. This needs to be recognised in employee communications. People want to know what 'their' organisation is up to and they also want to relate to this at a personal level. Their interest in the fact that, for example, a major export order has been won is at least twofold: the fact of the order and its effect on the organisation as a whole and them in particular is of interest. Also of interest is who, among their colleagues, has achieved this order and how. Employee communications need to straddle this double interest which is quite distinct from externally directed communications activity – the prime reason why it is so difficult to produce a newsletter which is suitable for both internal and external use.

There are a number of standard tools of the trade used in employee relations programmes which are worth looking at briefly and which should be considered in setting up such a programme.

Before looking at these, however, there is one point which should be made. Any public relations programme must have objectives and employee communications are no different. In setting out to inform and, perhaps, persuade, one is greatly helped if one knows where one is starting from so a communications audit (as discussed in Chapter 6) is a logical starting point and nowhere is it easier to conduct such an audit than within one's own organisation. What sort of programme is instituted and which tools of the trade are selected should be based on the findings of such an investigation.

119

THE NEWSLETTER

Newsletters can be produced at very different levels of complexity, from desk top published A4-sized publications through to a fully-fledged newspaper. As a means of internal communication they have the advantage of allowing one to mix news about people with corporate news and information, underlining the close relationship between an organisation and the employees who are its members. They provide a means of circulating corporate messages in a much less formal way than through official internal memos and with a chance to explain some of the background to decisions and actions taken. In large organisations where many of the staff rarely meet senior management they provide a chance to provide a personal face for 'the bosses'. They are, in short a first-rate way of communicating internally on a mass basis and in a reasonably informal and personal way.

Although little value in smaller organisations, partly because there is much less need for them where everyone knows everyone else and partly because they tend to be an expensive way of communicating to small numbers, in larger organisations the production of an internal newsletter has become standard business practice.

If an internal newsletter becomes too obviously a mouthpiece for management it greatly loses its effectiveness, but if it becomes too independent it may also become less effective as a communications channel, so the trick is to strike a balance in content, style and presentation.

Although it adds to the cost a good idea is to distribute a newsletters to the employee's home address. Not only is it then read in a more relaxed environment than the workplace, but it is made available to other members of the family – a strengthening of family ties to an organisation and an exercise in community relations.

NOTICE BOARDS

Mundane as they may seem, notice boards can be an extremely effective means of internal communication provided they are used imaginatively. The type of information which can be carried in addition to normal work announcements, club meetings and the rest is varied but has in common that it is designed to foster a sense of belonging and an identification with corporate aims and activities. It is also the sort of information which is unlikely to get posted unless the public relations function makes it its business to do so. Typical items might be:

- regular posting of press releases issued and press coverage traced concerning the organisation
- 'pulls' of any advertising campaigns which are running for the organisation, its products or its services – flag these up in advance so employees know about them before 'outsiders'
- news of particular achievements which may eventually appear in the house newsletter but which can be posted more immediately and made more locally topical on a site-by-site basis
- early announcements of senior appointments – don't let your

staff read about it in the *Financial Times* or hear it on the grapevine first.

In fact one can go a step further and create a 'wall newspaper' which becomes a special notice board for just such items and which can be presented along the lines of a blown up newspaper format – an easy task with today's desk top publishing systems and photocopying enlargers.

ANNUAL REPORT AND ACCOUNTS

Shareholders receive an annual account of how their company is doing, presented glossily and packed with information for those who can understand a balance sheet and commentary understandable even by those who can't.

A company belongs to the shareholders but, in many senses, it belongs to its employees too. The Annual Report and Accounts or, better still, an alternative version of it geared to the interests of employees, can usefully be distributed internally as part of employee communications.

121

COMPANY MEETINGS

Internal meetings can be an important part of internal communications and a valuable public relations exercise. They should be looked at seriously with this in mind and used to provide a regular channel of communication, not just called on special issues. It's also worth considering supplementing these with internal video presentations on particular issues which can be used for line management briefings and discussions in organisations which are too large to hold centralised meetings.

All these are ways of communicating downwards – from management to staff – but in any real communications system there will be upward and sideways communications too, covering everything from suggestion schemes to quality circles and from social club announcements to articles for sale advertisements on notice boards.

There are no particular PR techniques to ensure this upwards and crossways flow of communication since they will result largely from the operational practices of an organisation. However, it is a very real PR consideration that people should feel that they are not just being talked at but also listened to and it should be part of the PR function, if only in the role of facilitator, to ensure that this is the case. Thus, even if a suggestion scheme is introduced for commercial reasons it should be encouraged and winners publicised for PR reasons; even if a newsletter's prime purpose is to disseminate corporate messages and a cross flow of information, it should also allow for letters to the editor and, perhaps, classified advertising.

Community relations activity

When it comes to community relations the approach is, of course, rather different to employee relations but it is also rather different from the rest of the external public relations activities which one carries out. Techniques, though, are often very similar. For example your local press will have the same needs as the media anywhere, but the 'angle' at which they see a story and the degree of interest will be greatly influenced by the fact that you are a local organisation. Your may have a need to win acceptance for your business practices from ecological or conservation groups on a national basis, but you can be very sure that the debate will be a lot more heated and personal in your own back yard.

The particular aims of a community relations programme will depend on specific circumstances but will, in general, be geared towards ensuring that an organisation is integrated into its local community, with a degree of mutual respect and understanding and consequent benefits in all relationships from recruitment to planning permission.

It is not possible for public relations activity to create a positive relationship with the community which is not deserved. It is possible for sensible PR to ensure that an organisation gets the best reputation to which it is entitled and it is possible that PR considerations may influence the degree to which an organisation acts as a 'good neighbour' in terms of supporting community initiatives – theatre, charities, community centres etc. Certainly there should be a serious PR input when management considers what actions it will take within the community and such input should be given proper weight when considering time, effort and money spent through such local support, corporate involvement in local activity, provision of facilities etc.

People want to know, understand and, if possible, take pride in what happens in their locality. Community relations work is mainly geared towards letting this happen and to do so through a free flow of information. Over and above general PR actions undertaken at a local level – media relations, local sponsorship, and the like – there are a number of specific extra activities which may be worth considering.

123

OPEN DAYS AND VISITS

A natural curiosity about 'what goes on behind the gates' among neighbours and employees' families can be satisfied through open days and group visits, with great opportunities to show samples of an organisation's achievements and triumphs at the same time.

LOCAL PRESENTATIONS

There are always influential local bodies whose members are clear opinion formers in the community – from Rotarian to Women's Institute, and from Round Table to the local Chamber of Commerce. The opportunity should be taken to make presentations to such bodies about who you are and what you do. It informs and it shows you care about their opinion.

SPECIAL PRESS FEATURES

It's not usually practicable or possible to produce a special information sheet or newsletter for the local community (beyond home distribution of employee material as mentioned above), but you can use the local press to do this once in a while in a way which goes beyond the normal press relations programme.

Where you are an organisation with some importance in an area then special features become possible to organise on a fairly regular basis. Supported by advertising they are profitmakers for the local press, who will be pleased, and provide a channel for disseminating information in more depth than through standard media relations to your local public.

FLAGGING UP THE ROUTINE

It goes without saying that you will want to publicise any special initiatives which you take in your local area, but remember that the apparently routine is news too. Information about employees, probably researched for the employee newspaper is also of interest to the local press and reminds everyone that you, and your staff, are part of the community. News of your sports teams has a similar effect as does anything which helps put a personal face on an organisation in an area.

LOCAL COUNCIL

Strictly speaking, your local council may be regarded as part of the public for any public affairs activity which you undertake but it has a very important community relations element too. Quite apart from it making good sense to get to know the people who will make decisions on building planning permissions and all other local regulations which may affect you, local councillors tend to be important opinion formers in a community and keeping them informed of what you're doing is just plain common sense.

Community relations is not simply a matter of PR, it's a matter of concerned business practice and most responsible organisations recognise that they have a duty of concern to the community in which they operate. PR can provide the perfectly legitimate benefit of ensuring that you get full credit for the exercise of such duty of concern, and perhaps even a little extra.

20

Westminster, Whitehall, Brussels and the local council

'**P**ublic Affairs' is the name given to the specific PR discipline which concerns itself with government, at its various levels and with the various legislative processes which may have an effect on an organisation or business. It is one of the fastest growing sectors of the PR industry, together with Investor Relations and Crisis Management (discussed in the next two chapters), and it can involve the application of highly specialist skills based on extensive knowledge and a network of contacts.

Unlike in the USA, Britain does not have a formal structure of lobbyists (our reference to the lobby applies to journalists and the peculiar set of rules under which lobby correspondents operate) but, in effect, the work carried out by public affairs specialists is very similar to American lobbyists.

It may all seem very grand and when one hears of a question being asked on the floor of the House of Commons which has clearly been prompted by the activities of some special interest group one may be tempted to think, 'There's a fine piece of public affairs activity at work'. In fact the odds are that if the issue has reached open debate on the floor of the House then the cause is already in deep trouble.

There are a whole host of ways in which government action may impinge on an organisation and ways in which the administrative actions of Whitehall, the Eurocrats in Brussels or one's local council can directly affect business. Dealing with and reacting to these various forms of legislation can stretch way beyond concerns of PR and it is certainly way beyond the scope of this book to discuss the range of the relationship between business and government.

The specialists in public affairs are normally exactly that – specialists. They normally employ people with an intimate and direct knowledge of the workings of Parliament and of the Civil Service and typically include ex-MPs or political party employees in their staff. They may also have a number of current Members of Parliament attached to them and paid retainers to be 'consultants' or 'non-executive directors'. MPs have to declare their commercial interests but, having done so, they can act fairly openly on behalf of clients and a number of back benchers, mainly from the ranks of the Conservative Party, have links with various PR firms which offer public affairs services to their clients. In practice the value of the expertise which good operatives in the public affairs field have to offer is usually much more to do with knowing their way around Whitehall and the various committees of the House of Commons than it is to do with any spectacular performance during Parliamentary debates.

Just as with Westminster, so too with the European Community where a knowledge of how things work within the labyrinthine corridors of bureaucratic power is the main qualification for providing a public affairs service to clients. This normally means that one should look askance at anyone offering to deal with EC issues on one's behalf if they can't offer a Brussel-based operation for liaison and contact with the legislators.

Anyone whose actions and attitudes can affect the wellbeing of an organisation is a legitimate target for PR activity. If you're in a business where elected representatives or civil servants are likely to take decisions which may impinge on your wellbeing then it is certainly worthwhile making some effort to ensure that a degree of 'mutual understanding and goodwill' exists.

MPs, Euro MPs, civil servants, local councillors and council staff will be influenced by PR activities which you carry out simply by being members of the public. They read what the media has to say about you, may be directly aware of your products and company performance, may well have read some of your corporate literature and the like. The decision which one is likely to have to take is whether this limited amount of activity is enough or whether special efforts need to be made to win the understanding of some or all of these groups.

It's a decision which will depend on how important they are to you and, if the answer is that they may well be very important indeed, or if you can identify particular issues over which you wish influence them, then it will probably prove worthwhile ensuring that you have some professional help in dealing with them. Influencing European legislation, for example, is probably best not attempted on a do-it-yourself basis by someone with no knowledge or experience of the field.

128

On the other hand, most people are not too directly involved in major issues of public policy for too much of the time and for these people or organisations the need to influence the views of people involved in government is much more limited. At this level it simply makes sense to identify who the people of possible interest are and make some effort to keep them informed of what you are doing at a rather more intense level than with ordinary members of the public – after all they are influencers of opinion and you never know when you may need their help.

Routinely maintaining contact with one's local MP and Euro MP and getting to know them personally, keeping MPs with special interest in your area of business (easily identified from membership of special interest groups and, more complicatedly from checking past parliamentary questions in Hansard) informed of anything which they may find of value, making efforts to show involvement with your local council through dialogue and through community relations initiatives; all of these types of activity may pay dividends in the long term and are worth incorporating into your overall PR programme on a routine basis. It requires, after all, no more than identifying them as a target public at the start of creating a PR programme and then building in a number of formal activities which can be carried out in a relatively routine fashion.

If your need for liaison with these groups is more extensive than this fairly routine level or if you find yourself involved in a specific issue which calls for public affairs expertise then the best advice is to ensure that you have trained help. This help may be supplied through your trade association or its equivalent. It may be that you have the expertise 'in house' but not within the PR function – though this is unusual. It may well be that your local MP or MEP, as relevant, is prepared to go to bat on your behalf and make real efforts to co-ordinate a campaign because he truly believes in your case – job protection within his or her constituency, for example, will often gain great support if only because of the potential votes involved. Professional help can be bought in from specialist public affairs advisors and, since these companies are accustomed to working on a project basis, need not be excessively expensive.

129

A word of warning is, however, in order here. Public affairs has become one of the fashionable PR disciplines, rather like that other great consultancy money-spinner crisis management. As a result rather too many PR practitioners are claiming expertise in an area where their skills may be greater than the average man in the street but are not really expert. If one is really going to be involved in the business of public affairs then it is not enough to be a good all-round PR person who has gone out and bought a copy of *Dodd's Parliamentary Companion*; you need some specialist skills and knowledge.

It's worth checking out the true extent of public affairs knowledge and experience, together with a list of current clients, of any generalist PR firm you may be considering to work in this very specialist area. Some specialist lobby firms will refuse to reveal client names and you may feel that this speaks in their favour, as it may well do. You should still seek to gain some positive assurance of their activity and try to make sure that their contacts and effectiveness is not limited to one specialist area – some firms have very poor contacts outside the parliamentary Conservative party, for example, and they are not likely to be able to do much for you at a political level if you're dealing with a Labour-run local authority!

At the end of the day it's probably fair to say that lobby work is best left to the experts, as is any really serious public affairs issue with which one finds oneself involved. On the other hand, routine contact with all elected and employed officials does not necessarily require specialist help and can be carried out perfectly well by an organisation for itself.

For a large number of organisations a degree of public affairs activity is work which should not be ignored if only because this relatively small group of people, however venal and stupid we may sometimes think our elected representatives are, is an important one in influencing opinion and in affecting events which may very well have an impact on one's business.

21

Investor relations

For every publicly quoted company there is a key group of people whose understanding and goodwill is vital. They are, at the end of the day, the owners of the company. They are the shareholders. Some of these will be individuals and, fewer in number but greater in percentage ownership, some will be institutions.

Although they own the company they are, most of the time, separate from it. Their identification with the policies and views of the executive management cannot be taken for granted. Their interests are not identical with the interests of the company or at least if they are it is a matter of accident not of necessity.

A public company which does not ensure that there is solid dialogue with its investors, and this goes beyond the occasional face-to-face meeting with major corporate shareholders and the issue of an annual report to all shareholders, will, sooner or later, be likely to find itself with problems on its hands. It makes a great deal of sense to consciously work to win the understanding and goodwill of investors for one's policies and one's actions.

Now, for most reasonably large public companies, this is a massive oversimplification. There is no such thing as a static group which can be called investors. Shares change hands all the time. A large number of shares will be held by investment bodies, pension funds, unit trusts etc and these will have their shareholdings on behalf of a whole raft of indirect shareholders. Anyone active in the markets may be regarded as a potential shareholder and, as such, must also be communicated with. The share price of the company will be determined by trading which, in turn, will be greatly influenced by brokers and their analysts, by financial journalists and a range of financial advisors none of whom may actually own shares. Movements in the share price will affect the way shareholders perceive their company. A weak share price will invite takeover bids which will succeed or fail largely on the shareholders' view of the company and its management . . . and so on and so on.

Investor relations certainly needs to include elements of communications activity which are aimed specifically and directly at existing shareholders. It also needs to encompass the much wider world of the City as a whole in all its various manifestations and with all its special ways of working, its rules and regulations, its unwritten laws, its rumour mill and its network of interconnecting contacts.

It's a brave man, indeed, who sets out to mount a so-called investor relations programme without a map in his hand and a guide to steer him through the jungle; after all, everyone knows that the City eats interlopers for breakfast and that the analysts and journalists who stalk the 'square mile' are men of such penetrating insight and razor sharp intellect that they will only talk to established leaders of industry and makers of millions!

132

Actually, an awful lot of City PR is reasonably straightforward provided you know the rules and stick by them. In any reasonable-sized public company the rules which apply to issuing of information will be known by the Company Secretary at least – you can get into a lot of trouble if, for example, you go revealing price sensitive information such as performance projections to journalists without following the Stock Exchange regulations. By and large analysts and journalists want the same sort of information as any other type of commentator. It just happens that their area of interest is primarily financial rather than technical or commercial.

At least twice a year, interim and final results, there will be a focus of interest on your performance and in between times a varying degree of interest depending how active you are as a company, how much change there is in your trading conditions, how far you've entered the acquisition market etc. Providing clear and proper information at these times and supporting this by background briefings, issue of selective news stories and all the other normal elements of a PR programme is not frighteningly complicated and quite a few major companies feel perfectly competent to handle this from within, with a relatively small level of manpower devoted to the task.

At a purely mechanical level you do need to know who the people are who will be important to you in disseminating financial information, essentially financial journalists, analysts relevant to your business sector and the financial wire services. These, like most information contacts can initially be identified through the comprehensive directories which are available on the market (see Chapter 26). Of course, to do more than an absolute minimum job you need to spend some time establishing contact and a degree of understanding with key channels of information but this is simply a matter of time and effort. Provided you don't waste people's time and are seen to be a source of genuine value you do not need to be part of the City establishment or to have been to the right school or university. If this was ever true of the PR man working in the City it certainly no longer is.

133

Investor relations work is not limited to City contact, of course. A company's annual report is probably the most important corporate document it will ever produce and is an annually recurring key opportunity to present figures and policies in depth to shareholders and other interested parties. Direct communication with shareholders too provides opportunities to get messages across direct and undiluted by the intervening hand of journalist or analyst. Where there are a number of significant corporate shareholders it also makes sense to institute a programme, probably of personal meetings at board level, to ensure that they are kept comfortable with the way in which their investment is being looked after, and the AGM is not really the time or place to do this.

Mounting this kind of routine investor relations programme is not particularly hard, but it is time-consuming and it does require attention to detail and a fair bit of purely factual know-how. It is, sometimes, an activity which is left to the Company Secretary to carry out and normally when this happens it is a mistake. Journalists are not catered for. The importance of analysts is not fully recognised. Direct shareholder communications tend to be factually impeccable but totally lacking in anything which will engender goodwill and understanding. A PR input, if not total PR control, is normally of definite benefit.

Using a financial PR specialist for a routine level of City PR is another option and one which is not particularly expensive. One only has to look at the fee income of some of the leading City specialists and divide it by the number of their clients to see that a large number must be paying small fees indeed. One suspects that the service offered is little more than handling the announcement of final and interim results, placing some tombstone ads to coincide with these and issuing the odd press release but the fact is that City PR firms who are doing this all the time can carry through a basic programme very economically. They already know the journalists and analysts, can quote the stock exchange rules in their sleep, have standard procedures for calling analyst/journalist briefings and premises to protect the security of these and even have a formula approach to the production of annual reports and accounts which can save both money and heartache.

It may be felt that the use of such a basic City PR service is a good investment compared with the effort which is required to do it oneself but it certainly isn't necessary, no special or secret skills are required to do a routine job.

When it comes to a contested takeover bid, bringing a company to market, a share flotation, a tricky rights issue, however, the whole situation changes. Unless one has well-developed skills already available in house, a very considerable experience and knowledge base, a genuine network of valuable contacts, and the physical capability of handling the demands of a serious campaign under pressure, then it's total madness not to use specialist advisors to handle the PR for you, as a number of

134

companies have learned to their cost.

There are a number of PR consultancies competent to act for you in circumstances where intensive City PR work is needed. They are virtually all totally specialist in City work and they have cut their teeth on contested bids and flotation work. When the going gets tough it makes a lot of sense to have this type of specialist in your corner.

There is also a middle position for investor relations work which lies somewhere between the relatively routine and the kind of high pressure situation brought about by bids and offers. For a large number of companies there is a requirement to maintain a fairly high City profile on a continuing basis and this may be for a variety of reasons, usually connected to the share price but not necessarily so. In this situation corporate PR and financial PR tend to merge together and it is certainly the case that a programme needs to be managed with a fairly high level of expertise which means drawing on established skills and experience either through an in-house appointment or through taking outside advice.

135

More than most areas of PR, City PR tends to shroud itself in mystery and, given the proclivity of the PR industry as a whole to complicate the straightforward, that's saying something. However, it must be said that there are a number of specialists working in the field, both advisors and company employees, whose results are most impressive and could not be matched by anyone following the common sense rules and sensible planning which will suffice in many generalist areas of PR activity. It should also be said that City PR, like crisis management and to an extent public affairs, differs from general PR activity in one important respect. The consequences of getting it wrong can be out of all proportion to the extent of any mistake made.

It's certainly possible to handle most aspects of investor relations work oneself but if one does it is not something which one should take on casually or without giving it one's serious attention.

22

Crisis and issue management

The third big specialist PR area to have emerged over the past few years is crisis management which, essentially, covers the management of the public relations aspects of those serious events which have the potential to destroy, or severely damage an organisation's reputation virtually overnight. The type of situations typically covered by crisis management range from natural or man-made disasters to legislative problems, and from company scandals through to product recalls.

Awareness of the need to manage one's relations with various publics at time of crisis has been intensified by the observed commercial consequences of such high profile consumer product problems as the broken glass sabotage of baby food by consumer terrorists in the UK, the deliberate poisoning of the pain killing product, Tylenol, which resulted in seven deaths in the USA, and the contamination of Perrier Water which had a major impact on sales worldwide. Crisis management is not confined to consumer products, however, and a checklist of risk areas taken from the book *Reputation Risk Management* gives some idea of the range of potential risk areas with which crisis management PR concerns itself: *natural disaster; man-made disaster; product failure; product sabotage; information leakage; legislative risk; environmental issues; health issues; industrial relations; behaviour of high profile individuals; corporate/financial positioning; inaccurate media reporting; government action.* The list is probably not a comprehensive one but covers most possibilities for most companies. Organisations have been, and continue to be, seriously damaged by events falling under every one of these headings.

When crises hit companies the protection of reputation, the PR of the situation if you like, is rarely the first consideration of management. Nor should it be when there may be direct issues of threat to health or life involved. However, after the first impact of a crisis has passed it may well be a question of how well an organisation has handled its communications and protected against the threat to its reputation which has the longest and most profound effect on its wellbeing.

The PR techniques which one uses in a crisis situation, aimed at the protection of reputation and damage limitation, are not fundamentally different from those employed as part of the normal running of a PR programme. However, the circumstances under which they are employed, the time scales involved and levels of pressure experienced result in conditions which are radically different from the run-of-the-mill experience of running a PR campaign.

137

With the growth of awareness of the need to manage PR in crisis situations has grown a recognition that by itself crisis management is not enough. It is a last ditch technique resorted to when all else fails and, all too often, has to be grafted on to an organisational structure which is neither prepared or equipped to perform properly in the sort of crisis situation implied. So crisis management has expanded to include preparation for crisis, a sort of insurance policy designed to help manage the unmanageable in the unthinkable event that it occurs.

At the same time as preparing for crisis it's clear that it makes sense to take steps to avoid crises, at least as far as this is possible. One only has to think of the occasions when a controllable problem has turned into a disaster thanks to ill-considered management comment or inappropriate management action to see that some crises at least are avoidable. The management of situations where a potential, but far from certain, crisis can be seen looming on the horizon is widely referred to as issue management.

Both crisis and issue management involve PR skills being brought to bear within an organisation at a totally different level to product support PR, marketing communications or even a large part of corporate PR activity. They must be run as part of a senior management function and they must be given a high level of authority within an organisation if they are to be effective. For this reason the decision to become seriously involved in crisis management is not one which will be taken within the PR department but will be a main board decision (any crisis management programme which does not have main board backing and participation will be a waste of time). Similarly the decision to consciously identify and manage issues, either within or outside a crisis management programme, will also require agreement and commitment beyond the purely PR function.

An effective crisis management programme will have at least four main parts:

- identification of risk areas
- prevention of crises occurring (through issue management and, possibly, through procedural changes based on risk identification)
- preparation (a programme of preparing for the unavoidable crisis so that management is equipped to act quickly and in a prepared way when the unthinkable happens)
- crisis management itself.

These four aspects of crisis management go together to create what is increasingly being referred to as a 'Reputation Risk Management Programme', a description designed to underline that the whole purpose of the programme is the protection of the asset of reputation against damage and devaluation – with the obvious parallel with the type of risk management programme which might be put in place to protect the asset represented by company debtors. The steps are not dissimilar in that they involve seeking to minimise risk all along the way just as much as they seek to handle disasters when they occur.

Certainly the aspects of crisis management which have the highest profile are the handling of disasters when one feels that the specialists from the PR industry are rushed in to help deal with problems in much the same way that Red Adair is flown in to handle oil fires. This way of reacting is better than not paying attention to the communications and reputation demands of crisis, but it falls a long way short of being prepared in the first place.

The prime aim of a good crisis and issue management programme is to prevent crises occurring in the first place and a surprisingly large number of so-called crises are, indeed, avoidable since they are instances of organisations shooting themselves in the foot or they are examples of difficulties being allowed to assume crises proportions through poor handling by management.

The next most important element of a crisis management programme is to be prepared so that when disaster does occur you know what to do about it. Inventing a response to a crisis is really not done best under the pressure of events breaking all around you. In terms of reputation protection the first 24 hours of any crisis is critical and the one absolute rule of managing communication in crisis is to regain the initiative as soon as possible. You need to have everything ready, even though you hope you'll never need it, in anticipation.

139

Typically the preparation for crisis which should be undertaken will cover:

- identified crisis management team and alternates who will take responsibility for managing events, with clearly defined roles including those of acting as company spokesman as communications co-ordinator and as overall crisis management chair
- prepared sets of procedures to cover likely eventualities, actions to be taken as standard, detailed lists of contacts and communications channels
- physical support systems which will allow the crisis to be managed independently of the continued running of the organisation

- training and rehearsal for all members of an organisation who will have a role in managing crisis should it occur.

Obviously a great deal of detailed work is covered by these few bald headings and both the preparation for, and management of, a crisis deserves far more detailed discussion than is possible here. In essence one needs to establish a system by which everyone knows what they will do should a crisis break and, at the same time, one needs to provide a level of rehearsal and training which ensures that people are equipped to perform their roles and will stay level-headed and not throw the preparation out of the window when the real thing happens.

Crisis management is tricky. It is conducted under immense pressure when a crisis actually occurs and up to that time can seem like a waste of energy and effort. It is a set of circumstances in which the PR man has no second chances, he has to get it right first time and the consequences of getting it wrong are usually serious. For most people, whose organisation is not in permanent state of crisis, it is a form of PR of which they will have virtually no experience. The only people who do have experience of a number of crises are those who specialise in crisis management as consultants on the subject.

The conclusion is fairly clear. If you believe there is value in having a crisis management programme then get outside help at least to aid in setting such a programme up and, unless you really want to gamble at bad odds, don't wait until a crisis occurs but get a programme in place to make sure you're prepared.

23

Setting up a PR department

I hope that it's become fairly clear during the preceding chapters that PR simply isn't an activity which can be treated as a low-level support service which can be adequately done by junior staff with no training and little understanding of the organisation as a whole.

It's been argued that there is a great deal of unnecessary jargon surrounding PR and that there is a tendency for at least some PR operators to become both pompous and obscurist when discussing their trade. These should not distract from the basic simplicity of the business. The fact that a great deal of PR practice is not particularly difficult does not, however, mean that it shouldn't be seen as being important or that there is any justification for doing it badly. PR is not difficult in so far as it does not demand great intellectual capacity or a long and formal training. It does demand a fair level of attention to detail, good organisational skills, a fair level of intelligence and, above all, a clear understanding of what it should be aiming to achieve within the wider context of an organisation's overall goals.

All this means that setting up a PR department which will perform effectively entails rather more than simply picking a few reasonably personable individuals who don't have a critical role in some other part of the organisation and expecting them to get on with it. In practice this is what happens all too often where a likeable, but not over-effective, member of the sales staff is provided with a secretary, a limited budget and a reporting line to the marketing manager and told, 'Right, you're in charge of our public relations, and your first job is the Chairman's hospitality tent at the open golf tournament.'

We've looked earlier at how the PR function needs to be integrated into an organisation's overall structure and emphasised that PR does not operate in a vacuum but must have firm lines into the other complementary disciplines on the marketing communications front. If the expectation is that PR will operate fully at a corporate level then it is similarly important that the department should have proper access to corporate decision makers and knowledge of the context in which corporate PR should be carried out.

For large firms this can all lead to a large and extensive PR department, headed up by a corporate relations director, or similar title, with something close to board status and ready access at board level. Less grandly it means that, whatever the size of the organisation concerned or the size of PR department which is set up, there needs to be a direct line of communication from PR to board level – effectively there must be a head of PR, even if public relations is only a part of his or her responsibility, who is part of the top management team.

An in-house PR team can be large or small, not just depending on the size of the organisation involved but also on how much use is made of outside consultancies. But, whether the work is done through consultancies or 'in-house', a PR department will normally need the capability to perform a number of clearly defined operations and, as a minimum, needs to be equipped to do this. For simplicity these are divided here into three main sections which may be conveniently thought of as 'managerial', 'executive' and 'mechanical' although, in practice, there is liable to be some overlap.

MANAGERIAL FUNCTIONS

- identify corporate and marketing considerations which have relevance to PR activity for an organisation (these are liable to be extensive and, for a full PR programme, cover areas which are not immediately apparent; such identification is, therefore, likely to be a senior management function)
- create and budget an overall PR programme with clearly

stated aims and objectives, a defined strategy and specific programme of activity

- monitor the effectiveness of the programme and modify as necessary against achievement and against changing corporate aims

- prioritise activities within the programme to reflect corporate needs (this involves a continuous dialogue with other disciplines within an organisation and with senior management to ensure the integration of PR activity into the organisation as a whole)

- co-ordinate the overall operation of the PR programme, including the implementation of all external, particularly media, relations activity

- control budgets overall and on an activity by activity basis.

143

EXECUTIVE FUNCTIONS

The range of executive skills which will be required will, at least in part, depend on the scale and scope of the PR programme to be implemented. We have looked at a number of specialist areas of PR practice which may be needed in certain circumstances but which may have no relevance to some organisations. There are, however, a number of basic skills which will be required in any PR department which does not off load the entire PR programme onto outside consultants.

- writing capability is a necessity – a great deal of PR is about the spoken and written word and any department which cannot generate written material and cannot modify and sub-edit commissioned material will be short of an essential skill. (This might be regarded as another of the mechanical skills set out below but it is so central to PR work that to treat it as anything other than an executive requirement would be very misleading)

- management of suppliers – typically a PR department will be commissioning work from designers, printers, photographers, exhibition stand contractors, and a variety of specialist contractors, and the ability to provide clear briefs and to manage the relationships with such suppliers, including costs, is a necessity. This cannot be done without some knowledge of what is involved in the work which is being carried out and, even if one doesn't have to be an expert, it does mean that the department must know what is and isn't possible, what is and isn't important and what things should cost

- organisational capability/project management – a great deal of PR is about organisation and attention to the relatively detailed elements which go to make up a successful programme or event; if a PR function cannot take on board the management of such organisational complication on a continuing basis, then it will not be able to perform its function properly. Normally a PR department has to pursue a number of separate objectives, probably for a number of different masters, and drawing on a variety of sources of supply all of the time, therefore logistics skills are a necessity

144

- creation and implementation of any special programmes which are called for within the overall PR programme, for example crisis management, investor relations, is likely to call for outside support from specialist suppliers, but the responsibility for such activity will fall within the PR function and the executive skills to ensure that this can be managed properly will be a necessary capability for many organisations.

MECHANICAL FUNCTIONS

It is perhaps unfair to class these as purely mechanical functions; rather, they represent a list of tasks which, on a day-to-day level, a PR department may be expected to carry out. Some of these activities imply the existence of one or more of the managerial of executive skills mentioned above; some don't. Not all these tasks will be required of all PR departments; most will. Many of the tasks may be carried out by outside suppliers but will be the ultimate responsibility of the in-house department.

Within these bald headings there may well be a great amount of work and, implicitly, the exercise of a great deal of organisational and technical skill.

- maintenance of media lists – distribution of material
- provision of full media monitoring service
- establish and maintain full information files on all externally used communications material
- establish and maintain full photo-library
- establish and maintain full reference library on all special interest groups, important contacts and information channels
- organisation of events, including all logistics, guest lists etc
- provision of design, copy and printing service for publications (these may range from business cards to annual report and accounts)
- establish internal, two-way channels of communication for identification of specific PR needs and for necessary clearances on all actions taken and materials (press releases etc) issued
- control all budgets and relate these directly back to the agreed PR programme and costs.

145

From all this it can be rapidly seen that the PR function of an organisation is going to need a range of skills and a fair degree of mechanical back-up. Of course it doesn't follow that all of this needs to be supplied in-house. Some of it clearly will not be. For example, it makes a great deal more sense to employ a clippings agency to read for press coverage than to try and cover the whole field of publications and broadcasts internally, although you may want to set up a quick reaction internal reading service of key publications. Similarly it is unlikely that an internal PR department will contain anything other than the most rudimentary design capability – desk top publishing and some very simple graphics possibly.

Whether the capability is to be found in-house or bought in will make a difference to the number of staff on the PR payroll but, if one is to take PR seriously, it will not make any difference to the scope of activity which the PR department should be capable of carrying out. In theory a PR department may, and often does, consist of one person with some secretarial support. But this one person will have to have a high level of all round competence and access to a great deal of outside support. They will also have to be very senior in the organisation or have adirect line to the board and a line manager capable of managingthe PR function at a senior level, albeit on a part time basis.

In smaller organisations this requirement can be honed back considerably in terms of the amount of work required. It cannot be honed back to any significant degree in terms of the scope of the work to be carried through. Budgets may be smaller, the size of operations smaller, and there may be less optional extras but the same range of considerations applies to smaller organisations as to larger ones. PR requirements for a small organisation relate to those of larger bodies rather as a Mini might be said to relate to a Rolls Royce – they both require the same range of fundamental components and operate on the same general engineering principles.

146

Once this is recognised, the planning of a PR department is not so very difficult. It is simply a matter of ensuring that a general structure is arrived at which can perform all these functions. The level of staffing which will be required then becomes a decision to be taken on the basis of the anticipated work load levels for the department, and this depends on the size of the organisation, the level of importance which it is decided to give to the PR function and the degree of service which it is intended to provide to the various operating sections of an organisation.

This question of the level of service provided can be a tricky one in some respects. A PR department provides a service within an organisation and, as such, may be required to bring particular skills to bear to support any and all other sections of an organisation. This is typically what happens with a general publicity department and PR may get treated in the same way. This can have a seriously problematic effect particularly on PR which, if it is to be effective, needs to operate at a serious strategic level for at least some of the time. There is a real danger that a PR department which spends its time sourcing corporate gifts for the sales team, putting together a slide presentation for the manufacturing director, running small exhibition stands for regional sales operations, putting together presenter packs for brand managers etc becomes totally immersed in day-to-day problems at a fairly trivial level and loses the necessary perspective to manage overall PR effectively.

An in-house PR department needs to be set up in such a way that this difficulty is avoided. This almost certainly means that the PR function is clearly defined separately from the publicity function. Even if there is overlap and the same reporting lines the two activities should be kept distinct or, if not, combined into a marketing communications, 'marcoms' function with an appropriate level of staffing in seniority as well as numbers to   147
ensure that PR does not change from a service function to a servant function without authority and at the beck and call of everyone.

Some larger organisations have met this problem by making the PR department an in-house profit centre which charges out for its services internally when conducting work at anything other than the corporate level and which is, thus, not taken for granted and which has its size and scope of activity determined in part by a kind of play of market forces. This approach has had mixed levels of success but has worked for some organisations.

In practice, of course, it is unusual to find oneself developing a fully-fledged, full-service PR function from scratch. What normally happens is that a toe in the water approach is adopted and the PR department grows a bit like Topsy as the value of its contribution is appreciated. This is not a particularly good way of establishing a PR function, but it is the usual way. If this is the approach then there is one clear rule: *Start from the top down.*

If you try and build a PR department from the bottom up, for example by setting up a junior press relations officer as your starting point, then it is unlikely that you will ever manage to establish a really efficient operation (unless, of course you get lucky with the appointment and pick a genuine high-flyer who hasn't had time to establish himself or herself). The first appointment needs to be a senior one, whether it's an internal appointment or someone brought in from outside, and the head of PR needs to be given sufficient authority, access and scope of action to set out a proper programme from the word 'go'. Alternatively the responsibility for PR needs to lie with an existing senior member of staff who may not have detailed knowledge but who understands the importance of managing one's PR and the basic techniques. Any other PR appointment should then be clearly seen as support staff.

If PR is not allowed to be seen at a senior level internally then it won't work externally. So whatever you do in setting up a PR function, don't do it half-heartedly and don't do it on the cheap.

24

Using a consultancy

Using a PR consultancy to handle some or most of one's PR needs has become the norm rather than the exception in British industry and is becoming increasingly common in non-commercial organisations with PR needs such as charities, local authorities, trade associations etc.

There are a number of reasons for this, of which the most compelling is that, by and large, consultancies do the job better than in-house operations – though there are numerous exceptions to this resulting from outstanding in-house practice or poor consultancy performance.

The reasons why consultancies do a better job are, themselves, numerous but it is worth looking at some of them since they give some indication of why one might choose to go down the consultancy route rather than invest in a full-scale PR operation within one's company. The claims made by consultancies are open to debate, of course, and are offered here as objectively as possible, given that the writer has spent most of his working life on the consultancy side of the PR fence:

- Consultancies provide a pool of knowledge and experience which it is impossible to match in an 'in-house' department. All of the skills contained in a consultancy can be brought to bear on a client's needs as required.
  True in theory, except of the one- and two-person firms, but not always true in practice. The theoretic availability of all consultancy staff sometimes comes down to a small account team involved all the time and minimal input from other practitioners not directly involved. Benefits are only really

apparent when a consultancy takes the notion of pooling experience seriously and, while some do, some don't.

■ Consultancies provide a flexible resource which simply cannot be offered by in-house facilities.
Not quite the same point as the 'pool of experience' argument although related to it and, in this instance, almost certainly true.

■ Consultancies approach PR from an objective position and are not trapped in line management problems. They have this advantage in common with all outside consultants but, since they also implement programmes, they do not suffer the consultant disadvantage of power without responsibility.
By and large true. PR activity may suffer from being treated as a second rate activity within an organisation, not because of any conscious decision but because it does not obviously contribute to the bottom line.

150

■ By virtue of the fact that consultancies work for a variety of clients they have a wider perspective and a great deal wider experience than can be gained in-house. This is true of consultancies as entities and of the individuals employed in them.
Undoubtedly true but the price to be paid for this may be a lack of detailed knowledge and absence of focus. It's certainly reassuring to know that any individual consultant has gained some experience in-house at some stage in his or her career.

■ Consultancies have more efficient, dedicated systems geared entirely to the effective implementation of PR programmes.
True as a rule, but only because many in-house departments either haven't taken the time or spent the money to build equivalent systems.

■ The best operators in PR are drawn to consultancies rather than to in-house practice so it is in consultancies that you find the real PR talent and dedication.
Very debatable, though it is true that at most levels of seniority consultancy work pays better than in-house and that consultancy work is usually much more varied than in-house practice.

- Consultancies practise PR. This is their *raison d'être* and their sole concern, whereas for in-house practitioners PR is often simply one aspect of their job.

  True enough where an organisation hasn't got a dedicated in house PR function, but not an argument to prefer appointing a consultancy to setting up one's own specialist department.

There are also a number of arguments used against employing PR consultants and, again, they may have some validity.

- Consultancies are immensely expensive for what they deliver.

  Consultancy fees can certainly sometimes appear high at first sight but if one makes a comparison between the real cost, inclusive of related overheads, of setting up an in-house operation then the discrepancy is not so great. More importantly if one compares the quality of service and level of expertise gained from a consultancy with what is provided in-house then the costs normally compare favourably. Value for money rather than the cheapest option is the only reasonable way to judge consultancy fees.

- No consultancy can ever understand my business as well as my own staff.

  Probably true but you employ consultants for PR expertise and objectivity, not for being able to recite your stock list in their sleep.

- We can carry out our own PR better and less expensively than any consultancy.

  This may be true and, if it is, you'd be mad not to.

- Our PR needs are limited and the budget doesn't stretch to using a consultancy.

  Certainly one can carry out quite a bit of effective PR without using a consultancy or setting up an expensive in-house department. Where this is the limit of one's requirements then looking for outside help makes little sense except, perhaps, for one off help in developing an initial programme – a service offered by some, usually smaller consultancies.

- PR people are like all consultants – they charge a fortune, have no real involvement in one's business and finish up by asking to borrow your watch in order to tell you the time.

Nonsense. There are crooks, con men and flim-flam merchants in almost any business and PR consultancies certainly have their share. However all successful PR consultancies are built on the principal of retaining clients year-on-year and they don't do that without a commitment to service and delivery of value for money.

At the end of the day the decision whether or not to use PR consultants is probably influenced by a number of factors, including some, such as convenience, which have not been referred to in the preceding arguments for and against.

It is unlikely in the extreme that the choice to use a consultancy will be motivated by a desire to save money. By taking the decision to employ consultants either instead of or in support of an in-house function then one has made a commitment to investing in effective PR activity and has, implicitly at least, recognised the importance of managing one's PR in a serious way. There's little point doing this unless one is prepared to put in some effort to ensure that one's investment is a cost-effective one and this means working to ensure that one's consultancy is capable and allowed to act effectively on one's behalf.

There are certainly a large number of PR consultants around eager to win business and prepared to offer an extensive range of services within the overall banner of 'PR'.

There are probably some 1000 or so PR consultancies in the UK, ranging from substantial organisations which may be part of multinational advertising and PR groups to one person operators handling a limited number of clients from a converted spare bedroom in their homes. The PR industry's main trade journal publishes an annual listing of the 'Top 150' consultancies, though not all consultancies submit figures for inclusion. For the calender year of 1992 the largest consultancy showed a fee income of £23,400,000 and a staff level of 385 serving 452 clients; the consultancy filling place 100 had a fee income of £435,000 and a staff of 14 serving 18 clients.

It isn't just the total fee income which varies hugely from consultancy to consultancy but also the hourly rate on which fees to individual clients are based – a difference which is not always reflected in the level of service provided. The scope of services offered varies considerably too with some consultancies claiming to be all things to all men, and perhaps achieving it, and others offering a very precise range of services, possibly limited to a single area of specialisation such as public affairs or investor relations.

None of this is particularly surprising since PR consultancy is a typical service industry essentially selling time and capability. PR people have worked hard to achieve 'professional' status and, while it may be debated how far they have truly achieved this, the structure of the consultancy industry mirrors that of accountants or solicitors fairly closely, given that PR firms rarely act for individuals and, by and large work on a retainer or large project basis, rather than through large numbers of comparatively small transactions.

153

What the disparity in size of the various consultancies does indicate is that there is a lot of choice out there when it comes to picking a PR consultancy and that anyone seeking to work with one should choose carefully in order to get the right 'fit' in terms of skills, fee levels, personalities and working practices.

Using a consultancy effectively is as much a matter of selecting the right consultancy in the first place as it is a matter of the systems and practices which are set up for working. A good working relationship between a PR consultancy and its client is always dependent on there being a good level of personal understanding between client and consultancy staff working on the account. This doesn't necessarily mean that they need to like each other greatly, though it usually does, but it does mean that they need to understand each other and be able to communicate clearly and with mutual understanding.

If you don't like the people then it's unlikely you'll get a good consultancy service. If there is a poor fit between your expectations and what they have to offer then you definitely won't get a good service. If they are either too small to cope with your needs or too large to take you seriously as a client then you're unlikely to stay working together for long. If they don't have at least a broad understanding and experience of your industry sector then there are likely to be problems – but it should be said that it is far more important that PR people understand PR than anything else, just as a lawyer needs to know the law first and his client's business second. If there is a major discrepancy between what you expect to pay and they expect to receive then, again, the relationship is liable to founder.

It normally makes sense to talk to a number of consultancies before deciding who you want to work with and it also makes sense to ensure that these discussions are reasonably structured so that you can compare between what they are offering.

154

It is then reasonable to ask one or more consultancies to pitch for your business and most consultancies will be prepared to produce an outline of their approach to work on your account as a pitch document for which you will not be charged. No more than three consultancies should be asked to prepare such a proposal both because it is unreasonable to expect them to put in any serious work unless there is a fair chance of winning your business and because it becomes almost impossible to judge more than three presentations at one time.

The best time to establish what you expect from a consultancy and how you expect to work with them is at this very early stage. The preparation of a good, clear briefing document for the pitch is the best way of making sure that you have given all consultancies a fair chance to tell you what they can do and also of making it clear from the outset what your expectations are.

Just what the document covers is very much up to you. One reason for using a consultancy may well be that you are looking for *them* to tell *you* how PR can most effectively be run on your behalf and this will mean that you cannot spell out objectives, messages or possible tactics in any detail. As a rule, however, you should include everything you can which may be relevant, and which can be revealed without breaching confidentiality, about your business. You should give some indication of expected budget spend. You should outline preferred methods of working and indicate the reporting lines which the consultancy will have to work to. Most importantly you should provide the same brief to all consultancies competing for your business to allow them to pitch on a level playing field.

When it comes to actually choosing between the various candidates for your business there will be a number of different factors which will determine the decision, and these will vary from organisation to organisation. How well they respond to the brief, personal chemistry, knowledge of your industry sector, range of contacts, support service capabilities, international links are all factors which have been flagged up in surveys of the basis on which appointments are made. Really the only person who can sensibly prioritise reasons for choice is the particular client involved because he or she is in by far the best position to judge what is important.

155

There are a few things to check up on at presentations beyond the apparent reasons for choice which are worth mentioning, however, if only because they are often missed in the drama of the presentation. For someone considering appointing a consultancy for the first time a few tips may be of help:

- establish who is actually going to be handling your business – all too often the high-powered team which makes the presentation contains a number of members who you may not see again until it's time to discuss renewal of the contract

- clarify the precise basis on which proposed fees have been calculated and what amount of executive time, by which people, of what seniority is being allowed for

- check up on what, if any, hidden extras lurk in the proposals – what level of mark-up is operated on rechargeable costs, for example

- find out what, if any, ideas the consultancy has for measuring its own effectiveness and whether it has any systems in place for measuring its work for other clients

- check out the consultancy's client list and establish whether they are prepared for you to talk to any of their clients.

None of this will guarantee that you pick the best consultancy for the job or that the relationship will prove a successful one. Only practice will test this out properly. They will, however, make sure that you avoid a clearly inappropriate appointment, and the fact that you take this degree of trouble will help keep the consultancy on its toes from the outset.

Once you have a consultancy on board it is as much up to you to make sure that you get value for money as it is up to the consultancy to provide it to you. It's perfectly reasonable for you to expect the consultancy to push things forward and to be pro-active in its approach to your work, but at the same time it is not reasonable to expect them to work in a vacuum. When consultancy-client relationships break down or never get off the ground it is as often the fault of the client as it is of the consultancy.

One important element in ensuring that both consultancy and client succeed in working well together is to ensure that formal structures for reporting and monitoring activity are instituted from the word go. A consultancy will normally want to institute formal structures for itself, and if it doesn't you might want to ask why. You should make sure that these include:

- contact reporting of all meetings by the consultancy
- regular, formal review meetings between client and consultancy (in addition to day-to-day work meetings) probably at monthly intervals and supported by a status report which covers all PR work in hand (this status report, which may equally operate as the contact report of the formal monthly meeting, is a key document which enables responsibilities to be precisely allocated between client and consultancy and which tracks the progress of the various activities which go to make up the programme)
- clear reporting lines between consultancy and client which identify prime points of contact and lines of communication on both sides, including clearance procedures for any

material issued on your behalf

- precise agreement on billing procedures including, ideally, a monthly indication of hours spent on your work even if the relationship is a fee-based one.

These formalities will not make the relationship work well by themselves. They will create a structure within which good effective work can be done, provide a basis for co-operation between client and consultancy and provide an early warning system to prevent things going wrong unnecessarily.

Any consultancy worth its salt will want more than this. It will want the opportunity to integrate itself thoroughly with your organisation and it will want access throughout your management structure. This is reasonable and if you want to use your consultants as more than just some extra arms and legs you will make sure that they get the chance to act fully as advisors as well as doers. You'll probably be paying for a consultative service, not just secretarial and writing support, and the best way of making sure that you get value for money is to allow your consultants to do their job.

157

Most successful client/consultancy relationships are built up over a number of years and, without doubt, there is much more to be gained by building a long term relationship than by chopping and changing every few months. Remember every time you appoint a consultancy there's bound to be an element of paying for a learning curve, and the more thoroughly a consultancy understands your business the more able they are to advise you, sort out priorities and act as an extension of your organisation.

Of course, consultancies do get stale and sometimes a change becomes necessary simply to inject new ideas and new enthusiasm. By and large, though, the rule is to try for a long-term relationship. This is in the consultancy's interests too. Both sides benefit and both sides need to invest in making it work.

25

The things these people get up to!

There's usually a fair bit of talk about 'creativity' when the subject of PR comes up and much of the time such discussion is spurious in the extreme. 'Creativity' is all very well but, perhaps sadly, most of the time-effective PR is achieved through logically thought through programmes of activity based on clearly defined objectives. Success comes from a combination of organisation, attention to detail and a level of creative activity which is probably most accurately described as craftsmanship. 'Creativity' in the sense of the one-off, brilliant idea is merely the icing on the cake. Indeed such one-off ideas are rarely original but are usually simply reworkings of previous activities which have worked in the past.

Effective PR is not based on stunts. It is not based on single publicity coups. It is not based on empty-headed enthusiasm but on serious, structured planning and execution.

Having said this, and fully established one's credentials as a wet blanket and pompous ass, let's recognise that it is that element of something extra which we might want to call 'creativity' which can lift a PR programme from the merely competent into the outstanding.

Awards for excellence in PR practice, the Institute of Public Relations Sword of Honour, The Public Relations Consultant's Association Awards, The PR Week Awards, don't go to the one off creative idea, or at least very rarely. But it's these ideas which are remembered and which, frankly, are the most fun to carry out.

This chapter is intended as something of a diversion and as a cruise through a variety of PR ideas, some highly original and some relatively mundane, which have worked well and which no doubt will work well again.

In no particular order here is a rag bag of ideas, observations and mini-case histories which may prove useful in themselves or which may spark of the train of thought which leads to that something extra in a PR campaign. They're not necessarily the best examples, but they're ones which I've personally noted and found impressive. More important than the individual ideas, or groups of ideas, talked about is the approach which they illustrate and which may be helpful when looking for that extra something oneself.

The swearing parrot

Mark Borkowski is probably more accurately described as a publicist than a PR man; certainly he doesn't belong to anything as pedestrian as the Institute of Public Relations. When he decided to publicise *Treasure Island* at the Mermaid Theatre, his idea to audition hundreds of parrots for the role of Long John Silver's pet provided a first-rate photo opportunity for the media and useful pre-publicity for the show. His stroke of genius, however, wasn't the unusual audition call. It was to fire the parrot for bad language a few days later and, riding on the extensive publicity gained for the first audition, gain a whole second tranche of coverage which at least equalled the first.

If there's a general lesson to be learned here it must be that when you've got a good idea, milk it.

Branding the marathon

Mars took over sponsorship of the London Marathon in 1984. Previous sponsors, Gillette, had achieved some recognition of their backing but could not ever have been said to 'own' the event.

Mars recognised the simple power of branding, particularly in the finish area, and did two simple things. They heavily branded all of the slipover jackets of the finish marshals, of whom there are hordes around the finish area where TV coverage is concentrated. They provided clearly branded thermal metallic 'cloaks' for every finisher to wear once they'd crossed the line. The impact was astonishing.

Of course Mars did many more things to support the sponsorship but, to anyone who watched the race on television the visual power of the recurring marshals' jackets and, even more, the shimmering sea of Mars-branded thermal cloaks was tremendous.

160

After a single year's sponsorship Mars had achieved a spontaneous level of recognition of their sponsorship of the race which was 10 times greater than that previously attained – a significant number of people still believe that the London Marathon is sponsored by Mars more than five years after it passed into other hands.

If there are simple lessons here they are that sponsoring an event is only the start of one's commitment if you want it to work and that opportunities are always there if you look hard enough.

Lies, damn lies and statistics

Surveys have become a staple part of our way of life. Everything from election predictions to regional preferences in soft drinks are submitted to the enquiring gaze of the researcher and *the results are published*. It's perhaps too strong to suggest that when all else fails conduct a survey but it surely remains an immensely effective way of generating media coverage.

One of the quirkiest survey findings resulting in extensive coverage was conducted by the safety firm Bilsom who wanted to know why workers in high noise areas persisted in putting their hearing at risk by refusing to wear ear muffs.

Bilsom discovered that a small minority were worried about spoiling their hairstyle. The sheer triviality of the reason provided Bilsom with a news story which didn't just make the trade and safety press but found its way into the nationals, providing Bilsom with an opportunity to publicise its main products, which weren't ear muffs at all, but ear plugs!

Picture this

Picture stories offer some of the best opportunities for creative PR ideas and if the picture offered is strong enough in its own right it doesn't even need to have any real 'news' content. The 10-ton lorry resting on four perfect bone china cups said little about the product – nobody buys bone china for its surprising tensile strength – but what wonderful exposure for Wedgwood. The photograph of John Gummer and his child eating beefburgers probably did more to alleviate excessive public alarm over BSE than pages and pages of ministerial statements. Mark Borkowski, again, set up the photograph of 'fans' arriving at the West End production of *The Invisible Man* swathed in bandages and wearing dark glasses for a striking and very relevant promotional shot. Photographs of appealing baby animals, and new arrivals, seem to have been boosting attendances at London Zoo for ever, but why drop an idea which keeps on working just because you've used it before?

Pictures really do allow the imagination to have some room to move in. Children, cuddly animals, celebrities and pretty women are always good value but the potential is far wider than these tried and tested subjects. Contrasts usually work well, the very big and the very small or the very short and the very tall, as showmen from Barnum onwards have recognised. The genuinely beautiful works, so does outstanding photography in its own right, so does the truly dramatic. There aren't any real rules, though, that's why there's the chance to do something a bit different.

161

Competitive edge

Some of the best PR stunts have been based on competitions and one of the most effective of them all must be the annual search for Miss Pears. Although perhaps getting a little tired by now, the Miss Pears competition continues to gain its sponsors coverage year after year. How could it not with its obvious photo appeal and a positioning which continues to attract the attention of every proud mother in the country? More important still, from the point of view of effective marketing communications, is the perfect association between the product and the event. Pears hardly needs to say a thing about its soap – the fresh complexion of the winner says it all year after year.

If we contrast this with a recently claimed PR success for a jeans manufacturer promoting a 'Rear of the Year' competition we can see the importance of strong brand association for such events. Ignoring the somewhat dubious taste of the 'Rear of the Year' promotion (it did after all gain good press coverage for the jean-clad buttocks of an attractive young lady), one still has to query the value of the exercise from the sponsor's point of view. How good is the sponsor identification? Who did sponsor it? (As a matter of fact this promotion, which has run for some time now, is sponsored by FU jeans.) Would such a promotion not be more relevant where promotion of the generic can be justified through large market share. It may be that there are stronger benefits to FU than appear at first sight but if not this seems a classic case of the success of the event as a piece of promotion blinding everyone to the reason for doing it in the first place.

Still let's not try to stifle creativity with carping criticism and let's recognise the successful use of the competitive format (both for real competitions and simulated competitions of the 'best dressed man' or 'rear of the year' variety) from everyone from the bed manufacturer who sought out Britain's tallest man in order to demonstrate their range of bespoke beds through to *The Times* carefully low-key programme of PR around its annual crossword competition.

Generic promotion

Commodities and generic groups lend themselves well to PR specials and can often win media support simply because vested commercial interests are less obvious. Bottle banks apparently started in the UK as a result of PR initiatives by the Glass Manufacturers Federation. Fathers' Day was developed in its present form in the USA by the Tie Makers Association – a quite extraordinary piece of lateral thinking. Promotions for the Great British Sausage, the Beaujolais run for the new vintage each November, and numerous 'real ale' beer festivals are all examples of PR being usefully employed to boost sales of generic product groups.

Of course, if your market share is big enough, then it becomes economical to mount PR initiatives which support the market as a whole. Numerous 'advisory centres' and 'information bureaux', particularly in the food world, are no more than promotional fronts for one or a small number of manufacturers. The highly successful programme to encourage responsible pet ownership which has been driven by pet food giant Pedigree makes sense because of the degree to which the company dominates the prepared pet food market.

This type of PR creativity may not seem relevant to smaller organisations but it can work at a local level too. The bicycle retailer who mounted a clean air awareness campaign and got cars banned from the centre of his local West Country town certainly knew what he was doing!

Backing a winner

It's pretty obvious in the field of sponsorship that a shrewd choice of just what to support can pay very big dividends. If you're sponsoring an individual or a team it helps no end if they turn out to be champions – and can prove seriously embarrassing if they turn out to be no-hopers. Rather less obvious is the skill to spot when something has the potential to become of increasing interest to the public and to get in on the ground floor. Embassy's sponsorship of darts and snooker falls into this category where, in addition to the sports involved providing a good fit with the sponsoring product, the impact which has been achieved in terms of TV coverage is much greater than could have been imagined in the early days. Realising that colour television would result in the minimal TV coverage of 'pot black' being expanded into exposure of massive proportions may seem blindingly obvious now, but it was a shrewd judgement at the time.

It's not just in the sponsorship field that anticipating trends in interest or opinion can pay dividends. It would be wrong to suggest that organisations adopt business practices for PR reasons but recognising the PR potential of corporate practice and exploiting this potential is something which a number of companies have done superbly. The conscious positioning of Body Shop as trail blazers of environmental awareness has been a marketing and PR triumph, solidly based in the philosophy of the company's management but taking full advantage of the PR potential. In complete contrast the positioning of Porsche cars during the 'yuppy' 80s milked the prevailing attitudes of the young rich of that time to the full with a host of PR initiatives supporting this positioning. In both cases the companies were ahead of their times in spotting an attitude trend and exploiting it to the full.

Snowball effects which run and run

It can be a PR man's dream to set the self-renewing story running. The situation where the story takes on a life of its own and all the originator has to do is sit back, measure the coverage and, perhaps, inject the occasional boost. Of course this can also be the PR man's nightmare when the story is a negative one and is a scenario typical of poor or absent crisis management.

Some of the self-renewing stories which have taken on a life of their own are a little surprising.

A continuing discussion of the Mars Bar as a unit of currency started as an item in the *Financial Times* which pointed out that the bar, consistent in size and made up of basic commodities provided a consistent value for money and a measure of varied inflation (how many Mars Bars was a Rolls Royce worth in 1940 and how many today; what was a newly-qualified graduate's salary in Mars Bars in 1960 and what is it today etc.) The story ran and ran in the 'serious' press with very little effort from Mars and with a continuing reinforcement of the perception of the product as consistent and fundamentally sound.

Häagen Dazs ice cream made a considerable impact in the UK with its daring advertising, sensual and sexy. The ads had considerable impact but the editorial discussion which followed and which frequently reproduced the advertisements as editorial worked even better. Gold Blend achieved much the same PR coup on the back of advertising with the mini-soap series of advertisements which gained such editorial impact that the couple's first kiss gained front page coverage on the largest circulation daily newspaper in Britain. Both of these PR coups, sparked by advertising initially, took on a life of their own as discussion and dialogue in the media became self-fuelling.

165

Other PR initiatives which have taken on a life of their own include the 'I'm backing Britain' campaign launched by Colt in the 1960s; the extraordinarily successful RSPCA campaign for dog registration which created a massive debate in the media by running a fairly limited, but hugely controversial, advertising campaign focusing on the numbers of dogs put down in Britain each day; similarly successful campaigning PR mounted by Lynx in opposition to the fur trade where a combination of events and advertising fuelled a debate which took on a life of its own.

Self-generating PR 'snowballs' are probably most commonly found in the field of campaigning PR where particular pressure groups want to bring an issue to the fore and are prepared to go to considerable lengths to do so – the issue being all important to them and not simply a single aspect of their operations, also the issue being important enough to be a natural matter for public debate which only needs highlighting to come to the fore. It is not a phenomenon limited to issues, however, and when it is achieved by an organisation for its own PR objectives, whether they be commercial or corporate, then one sees PR at its most amazingly cost-effective.

Triumph from disaster

Keeping one's nerve when things seem to be going against one can actually be a recipe for turning disaster into triumph, or simply exploiting embarrassment. It happens all the time in the world of sport and entertainment – Eddie the Eagle, with his consistent failure as a ski jumper, became better known than any number of Olympic medal-winning performers and picked up a bit of sponsorship money too; the show-saving perform-ance of the talented understudy plucked from obscurity when the star is ill has become a show business cliché, which still grabs the headlines.

In the world of PR, something not so very different in terms of the potential embarrassment factor faced Lynn Franks, one of the industry's better known practitioners. Edina, the unspeakably awful heroine of the hit TV series *Absolutely Fabulous* which has been mentioned before, was widely reported to be based on Ms Franks. In the face of such publicity most people might be expected to crawl into a hole in embarrassment. Was this how Ms Franks reacted? Not a bit of it. She noted the title of the show, threw a part for her client Absolut Vodka, punning the title into the Absolut-ly Fabulous Party, and persuading the star of the show, Jennifer Saunders, to attend as guest of honour. A combination of creative thinking and sheer nerve which leaves one breathless and truly illustrates the sort of 'something extra' which separates the sheep from the goats in the world of PR.

People like Lynn Franks or Mark Borkowski are talented indeed and have both done a lot more in PR than just come up with some good ideas. Lynn Franks has also built a consider-able PR consultancy with a string of quality clients, clearly demonstrating that she can plan and conduct longer-term cam-paigns as well as come up with good ideas. Mark Borkowski has similarly shown staying power in the way that he has retained his show biz clients over time – though confining himself to show biz he claims he could come up with as many good ideas for coat hangers. Talented though they are, neither Borkowski or Franks is unique in PR and the fact that they are well known may be as much due to assiduous self promotion as to exceptional achievement. There are bright ideas which add an extra dimension to a PR campaign all around, some extra-ordinary, some apparently mundane but all producing an extra dimension.

You intend floating a company on the London Stock Exchange in the days when the floor of the exchange was still in one place and not dispersed across various dealing rooms. Although well known in its own sector, the company was little known by the boys in the City. How can you gain an instant City awareness in time for flotation?

The PR consultants involved suggested painting all the number 11 buses which ran through the heart of the City, from Liverpool Street and past the Stock Exchange, in the client's colours and logo.

Once done, awareness among the target audience, jobbers and brokers, arose 10-fold in a three-week period.

Wanting to launch a general sports insurance scheme to amateur sportsmen (mainly C2 socio-economic group foot-ballers), what do you do?

Get Ian Botham and Bill Beaumont, two of the most famously injured British sportsmen ever and stars of *A Question Of Sport*; put them with a pretty physiotherapist dressed in a variety of sport protection gear; write a serious story on sports injuries and their cost to industry. Put it all together in a photocall and you finish up with coverage in every national tabloid paper, television, provincial press and specialist sports magazines. You also sell a lot of insurance.

You're running a City conference on the eve of Budget Day. How do you make sure it hits the national media and makes your guests feel they've been at an event of national significance?

Invite an ex-Chancellor as your lead speaker, and brand the podium clearly with your logo. The inevitable spleen of a pre-Budget day speech by a yesterday's man is bound to make the national media – TV and newspapers – your guests feel that they were at a key event and your branding of the venue gives you national exposure without your ever seeming to push a particular company line (remember the advice on branding under photographic and TV coverage). Telerate, with the help of their consultants Sheldon Communications, pulled this off using Nigel Lawson on the eve of the 1993 Budget.

Knowing that the main media coverage of your sponsored athletic event will be a shot of the finish and you're not allowed to brand the athletes' vests, how do you brand the event?

Make the finishing tape three times as wide and brand it. It will be in every picture of the finish. (Morley, the knitwear people, did this back in the early 60s for 'The Morley Mile', with some help from their consultancy 'Voice of Sport'. This was at a time when the rules on athletics branding were Draconian.)

None of these ideas and anecdotes are likely to have a direct relevance to the everyday demands of a working PR man but I hope that they may spark a few ideas and give one pause for thought when planning a campaign – there's nearly always an extra twist that can be added with a little bit of extra thought.

26

Where to find out

This, the penultimate chapter of the book, is more of a listing than a chapter proper. It contains the sort of information which, in most management books is buried away in an appendix. From the very start of our discussion it has been argued that a great deal of PR is a matter of following a few rules, provided you have the access to the necessary factual information on who, how, where, why and when to actually make things happen. Knowing who to go to in order to get a list of particular types of journalist, knowing who can recommend a PR consultancy to you in an unbiased way, knowing how you can trace the press coverage which your work has generated; this type of information is vital and does not deserve to be buried away in an appendix.

The names and addresses listed here do not provide a comprehensive list but they cover a good deal of the ground and should prove helpful. Purely factual information or descriptive material issued by the organisations themselves is combined with some personal views. In order to make it clear where I am expressing a view of my own, rather than reproducing published information, all my comments within the listing are italicised.

The Institute of Public Relations

The Institute of Public Relations represents professional practitioners in the UK whether they work in-house or in consultancy. It is the sole body which regulates and represents individuals in the profession in the UK. The IPR was founded in

1948 and with over 3,600 members is by far the largest organisation of its kind in Europe.

The Institute aims to:

- establish and prescribe standards of professional and ethical conduct and ensure the observance of those standards
- encourage attainment of professional, vocational and academic qualifications
- provide advice, information and opportunities for discussion on all aspects of public relations work
- promote the development, recognition and understanding of public relations
- maintain contact with fellow practitioners in the UK and throughout the world.

For further information contact:

The Institute of Public Relations
The Old Trading House
15 Northburgh Street
London EC1V 0PR

Primarily of interest to people working full time in the PR business, or seeking to become full-time PR people, the IPR suffers from typical trade association syndrome in that it spends much time as a talking shop, contemplates its own naval rather a lot, and can be numbingly pompous when discussing its business. Nonetheless it provides a number of useful services to the industry and help to those wanting to know more, is the main spokesperson for the industry, tries valiantly to raise standards of professionalism and, in granting the status of MIPR provides the only objective measure of whether a PR person is at least reasonably competent.

The Public Relations Consultants Association

The Public Relations Consultants Association was formed in 1969. It is a trade association with 161 corporate members representing the majority of established consultancies in the UK. There are also nine overseas associates.

The principal objectives of the PRCA are:

- to raise and maintain standards in consultancy practice
- to provide facilities for government, public bodies, associations representing industry, trade and others to confer with public relations consultants as a body and to ascertain their collective views
- to promote confidence in public relations consultancy, and consequently in public relations as a whole, and to act as a spokesman for consultancy practice.

Further details are available from:

PRCA
Willow House
Willow Place
London SW1P 1JH

Obviously of main concern to PR consultancies, the PRCA also provides a computer-based referral service which can be of great value to anyone seeking to identify a suitable PR consultancy. A computerised system, not unlike a dating agency, will try to match requirements with member firms' areas of competence and will provide a suggested shortlist of not less than two and not more than five member consultancies for consideration.

The Communication Advertising and Marketing Foundation

The Communication Advertising and Marketing Foundation was established in 1970 to administer the examinations which, hitherto, had been conducted by separate industry bodies. The Cam Certificate Examination covers six different subjects and success in these six separate examinations achieves the CAM Certificate in Communication Studies. This is a prerequisite for sitting the CAM Diploma in Public Relations, which is necessary for membership of the Institute of Public Relations (MIPR).

Details can be obtained from:

The CAM Foundation
Abford House
15 Wilton Road
London SW1V 1NJ

Press cuttings agencies

There are a large number of press cuttings agencies, offering a variety of levels of service and a range of reading lists. Their charging structures vary too. You will know what sort of publications will be likely to cover your stories so check reading lists and ways of working before committing to any particular firm. These are some of the many people offering a Monitoring and clipping service.

Durrants Press Cuttings Ltd
103 Whitecross Street
London EC1Y 8QT

International Press-Cutting Bureau
224–236 Walworth Road
London SE17 1JE

PIMS Press Cutting Service
PIMS House
Mildmay Avenue
London N1 4RS

Romeike and Curtice
Hale House
290–296 Green Lanes
London N13 5TP

Definitely of interest if you have a public affairs need but not really a clipping service in the normal sense is:

Parliamentary Monitoring Services Ltd
19 Douglas Street
Westminster
London SW1P 4PA

Media guides

The term 'media guides' covers a multitude of sins from information about future features and supplements to essential advertising data. Here are some which have proved of value to me over the years.

ADVANCE THEMETREE LIMITED

173

Provides advance information of forthcoming editorial features and supplements in the UK and European press.

Advance Themetree Limited
2 Prebendal Court
Oxford Road
Aylesbury
Bucks HP19 3EY

BENN'S MEDIA DIRECTORY

Three different volumes covering the UK, Europe and the world. Lists newspapers, consumer and business periodicals, directories, television, cinema and radio, plus organisations and services to the media.

Benn's Media Directory
Riverbank House
Angel Lane
Tonbridge
Kent TN9 1SE

BLUE BOOK OF BRITISH BROADCASTING

A directory of broadcasting contacts for all radio and television programmes made within the UK.

Blue Book of British Broadcasting
Communications House
210 Old Street
London EC1V 9UN

Invaluable.

EDITORS

A six-volume regularly updated media directory with comprehensive listings of editorial contacts and publication profiles within the UK media.

Editors
Media Directories Limited
9–10 Great Sutton Street
London EC1 0BX

PIMS

Produce nine separate directories:
  PIMS UK media directory
  PIMS media town list
  PIMS european media directory – trade & technical
  PIMS european media directory – daily newspapers
  PIMS european media directory – consumer
  PIMS business investor & government relations directory
  PIMS USA media directory – trade & technical
  PIMS USA media directory – daily newspapers
  PIMS USA media directory – consumer

PIMS International plc
PIMS House
Mildmay Avenue
London N1 4RS

PR PLANNER

United Kingdom – a loose-leaf, continually updated media service on all UK dailies, radio, television and women's magazines.

Europe – a loose-leaf, continually updated classified directory of trade and technical journals and daily newspapers of 14 countries of Europe.

PR Planner United Kingdom
Hale House
290-296 Green Lanes
London N13 5TP

TWO-TEN

Comprehensive media directories covering the UK and Europe. Also Briton's Index of Investment Research Analysts.

Two-Ten Communications
Communications House
210 Old Street
London EC1V 9UN

Some producers of directories do an awful lot more than simply produce lists of who works where and what their copy deadline is. They offer a whole range of services which include printing and distributing your press releases, or sending them out electronically, or sending them over the wire (Two-Ten actually owns UNS which is a wire service with UK coverage to match PA and Reuters but distributing paid for releases). They will produce and distribute syndicated broadcast tapes; they will produce and distribute video releases; they have hand-delivery rounds to the national newspapers at regular intervals; in fact if you want they will take the entire mechanical side of media relations completely out of your hands and, at a price, do it for you. The range of services provided by Two-Ten Communications is, frankly, staggering and, while theirs is the service I know best, I understand that the added extras from others are also extensive.

BRAD DIRECTORIES & ANNUALS

Monthly directory of media facts including newspapers; consumer and special interest publications; business and professional publications; broadcast and electronic media; outdoor and poster media and advertising trade associations, societies and clubs.

Brad Directories & Annuals
Maclean Hunter House
Chalk Lane
Cockfosters Road
Barnet
Herts EN4 0BU

Of more value to advertising people than PR operators generally but still useful and providing detailed circulation and advertising rate data.

HOLLIS PRESS & PUBLIC RELATIONS ANNUAL

News contacts – commercial, industrial, consumer, professional, financial and corporate; official and public information sources; PR consultancies; reference and research addresses for communicators; services and suppliers and Hollis sponsorship contacts.

Hollis Press & Public Relations Annual
Contact House
Lower Hampton Road
Sunbury-on-Thames
Middx TW16 5HG

HOLLIS EUROPE

A directory of European Public Relations and PR Networks, providing consultancy listings in 30 countries; public affairs and government relations consultants and research and information.

Hollis Europe
Contact House
Lower Hampton Road
Sunbury-on-Thames
Middx TW16 5HG

The two Hollis directories contain a wealth of information beyond the listing of PR firms which forms the core of their content. Among other things, one can get a far more comprehensive listing of the various PR support services available by looking in Hollis than it is possible to provide here.

DODD'S PARLIAMENTARY COMPANION

Hurst Green
Etchingham
East Sussex TN19 7PX

177

VACHER'S PARLIAMENTARY COMPANION

Vachers Publications
113 High Street
Berkhamsted
Herts HP4 2DJ

VACHER'S EUROPEAN COMPANION

Vachers Publications
113 High Street
Berkhamsted
Herts HP4 2DJ

The titles largely speak for themselves – starting points if you want to know about politicians and the mysterious ways in which they go about their business.

Broadcast monitoring

If your need is for monitoring of news and current affairs programmes on regional, national, international and satellite radio and television networks then you're going to need the help of one or more of the following. It helps if you can give advanced warning of expected coverage but, then, if you know it's coming you can often tape it yourself.

CTC Telepictorials
13 Broadwick Street
London W1V 1FP

Newscan National Press Monitoring Service
45 Hendham Road
London SW17 7DH

Parker Bishop Ltd
4th Floor
2–6 South Street
Worthing
West Sussex BN11 3AE

Speedex UK Limited
51 South Molden Street
London W1Y 1HF

Tellex Monitors Ltd
The Broadcast Reporting Service
Communications House
210 Old Street
London EC1V 9UN

News agencies

There is no doubt that coverage gained through one of the independent news agencies gets widely used and is treated with respect by the media – something which is probably much less likely to be the case with a paid-for distribution provided through a commercial service. There are two major news agencies and these are very serious people, to be treated with at least as much respect as any other part of the media and with more respect than most.

THE PRESS ASSOCIATION

85 Fleet Street
London EC4P 4BE

REUTERS LTD

85 Fleet Street
London EC4P 4BE

Lots of valuable sources have been left out (you'll find most of them in Hollis as suggested above). Even within the categories listed there are omissions which reflect either my own ignorance or prejudices (no-one is included with whom either I or my company has had a seriously bad experience). Even so the above list should provide a fairly strong starting point and any PR person who is remotely serious about what they're doing will expect to have copies of a number of the reference works referred to on their shelves, and will have established working relationships with at least some of the services identified.

179

27

Conclusions

O ver the last 26 chapters we've skipped cheerfully through the world of PR, looking fairly seriously at some aspects, skirting over others when they seemed overly complex or specialised, setting down rules and guidelines where these seemed appropriate and trying to avoid these where they seem to be more inhibiting than helpful.

What may have become apparent, and it is certainly the intention that it should have, is that managing one's public relations depends as much on an attitude of mind as it does on being aware of a string of particular techniques. These techniques are necessary at the fairly simple level which has been largely covered in this book, but they are nowhere near enough in themselves. A grasp of what one is attempting to achieve is much more important than the business of learning how to achieve it.

There are huge numbers of people who would describe themselves as being public relations professionals who have never grasped this fundamental truth. And there are businessmen who have never given the formal disciplines of PR a second's thought and yet who instinctively operate on a basis which takes into account the need to inform and to win consent from their publics. Knowing about PR really isn't the same thing as being able to manage one's public relations.

It's not a great deal of use knowing that a press release should be written with the main story in the first paragraph if you haven't got a clue about what the media is likely to regard as being newsworthy. It's not much use having an exhaustive knowledge of how print processes work if you can't see what makes one piece of printed material effective and another useless.

We've tried to look at some of the most widely-used PR techniques and to provide mechanical guidelines, and some reference sources, to enable one to employ the basic techniques of public relations management for one's own organisation. Without the basic information and practical capability to implement one's intentions one is hamstrung. However without an understanding of 'why' a knowledge of 'how' or 'what' is only of value at the most basic and mechanical level.

Even the most careful reading of the previous chapters and a studious memorising of the 'rules', hints and comments made would fall a long way short of giving one a thorough background in PR. There are a large number of textbooks which provide detailed information on all sorts of detailed aspects of the business – seven rules for writing a feature article, everything you ever wanted to know about photogravure, the difference between thermofaxing and die stamping on invitation cards and the like. Unless your aim in life is to be a junior operative within a large in-house PR department of a multinational or a local authority, forget it.

A grasp of what PR is all about, and in particular an understanding that the building of reputation is an activity of great potential benefit, is a huge step towards the effective practice of PR and is of vastly more value than knowing the difference between a serif or sans-serif typeface.

Let's restate the basic principles which underlie everything which has been looked at in this book.

- although we talk about public relations as if it is an activity this is, in fact inaccurate; one has public relations whether one likes it or not. The choice one has is whether or not to manage these public relations in a deliberate way
- PR is essentially a matter of reputation and reputation is a matter of perceptions; perceptions can be true or false, accurate or inaccurate. Most importantly they can be influenced

- influencing the perceptions of those groups of people who are important to one is an exercise in 'establishing and maintaining mutual understanding and goodwill'
- in general the effective management of PR does not produce a direct effect, measurable in return on investment terms; what it does is to make everything which an organisation does easier to achieve. Thus, it creates an atmosphere in which sales are made; it creates a reputation which makes recruitment of quality staff easier; it allows one's arguments on issues to be listened to with sympathy etc
- although PR benefits are not to be perceived directly (with a few exceptions such as share price), they are real and should be looked at with the same type of questioning eye as any form of management activity
- PR need not be a vague and wishy-washy discipline but should be strictly planned and managed with clear objectives, clear strategies and clear budget commitment
- planning the programme, identifying objectives and working out a strategy is the hard part; all else is merely technique and, at least to a certain level of competence, is not inaccessibly hard or complex.

182

For the most part PR is an exercise in communication with people who are perfectly prepared to listen provided one takes the trouble to present one's messages in an absorbable, relevant and interesting form. This applies to the channels of communication, mainly the media, just as much as it does to the end audiences.

There is no real substitute for experience in running effective PR operations but the principles which one needs to follow are not difficult to understand and the information which one needs to achieve some level of basic competence is not difficult to access.

Provided one gets rid of the idea that PR is some form of secret or free advertising and sees it for what it is, a way of strengthening your position on all fronts by winning understanding and goodwill, and provided one is prepared to take some time and trouble over what one is doing then the implementation or management of a basic PR programme is a perfectly feasible thing to consider for oneself and the management of more complex programmes, using outside consultants or an internal department or both, is not excessively complex.

If you are not making a conscious effort to manage your organisation's PR, or if your efforts are limited to sending out product press releases in support of your advertising, then the chances are you are missing an opportunity. If the reasons for not managing your PR are because you believe it to be too complicated or too costly or not cost effective, then it's virtually certain that you are making a mistake.

183

Index

■